Sheffield

History and Guide

Sheffield

History and Guide

David Fine

ALAN SUTTON

To Polly and Jerome

'Some cities love their antiquities, Sheffield has few to boast of, and therefore treats them with scorn. Some day it will regret it.'

Sheffield Daily Independent, 1906

First published in the United Kingdom in 1992 by
Alan Sutton Publishing Ltd
Phoenix Mill · Far Thrupp · Stroud · Gloucestershire

First published in the United States of America in 1993 by
Alan Sutton Publishing Inc. · Wolfeboro Falls · NH 03896–0848

British Library Cataloguing in Publication Data

Fine, David
Sheffield: History and Guide
I. Title
942.821

ISBN 0-7509-0189-6

Library of Congress Cataloging in Publication Data applied for

Jacket Illustration: Sheffield Town Hall (*Sheffield City Council*)

Typeset in 10/13 Times.
Typesetting and origination by
Alan Sutton Publishing Limited.
Printed in Great Britain by
The Bath Press, Avon.

Contents

	Preface	vi
1.	The Place	1
2.	Origins	10
3.	A Village in Hallamshire	21
4.	A Cutting Edge	28
5.	From Manor to Manufacture	40
6.	Steel by the Yard	51
7.	The Turn of Two Cities	67
8.	From Rhetoric to Rust	75
9.	The Politics of Culture	87
10.	The Future	102
	Walking Tours: Introduction	109
	Walk 1: The Centre	110
	Walk 2: The Porter	114
	Walk 3: The Lower Don	115
	The Next Steps	117
	Acknowledgements	118
	Index	119

Preface

The history in this book is a guide to the past in just the same way that the walks at the back take you through parts of the city. It's not exhaustive: a blow by tilt-hammer blow, street-by-street history of Sheffield. It aims to give you a picture of how Sheffield developed, and still is developing.

In this it is a little different to most other histories. It runs past yesterday and the last of the old cream and blue trams, and into today, the building of the new Supertram, and the future beyond. History works by looking backwards at the past, but it does not have to stop there: time has no buffers, nor an end of a line. For Sheffield, a city of change, I believe as well as feel that it is particularly vital to look deeply into the future as well as the past.

And if history must repeat itself, then historians are surely the best-qualified of crystal-ball gazers! Here's where I admit my training is as an archaeologist: 1976 saw me start studying the subject at the university here. Consequently this book reflects an interest in landscapes and features as much as documents and meetings. It is a book of places rather than records.

It is not an insider's view. If you pick up a J. Edward Vickers or a Peter Harvey, almost any local history about Sheffield, you hardly need read the flyleaf to know these authors are born-and-bred Sheffield; that they could hardly spend a day without thinking of the city. I do not possess these credentials. Instead I have attempted to employ the distance of my personal origins to place Sheffield into a wider cultural map; to show how others see Sheffield as well as how Sheffielders see themselves.

Each chapter and each walk can be read separately, though they have been arranged in their natural chronological sequence. Feel free to duck and dive, or start at the end, treating the book as an archaeological dig!

To help fingers cross-reference between chapters and walks, appropriate page numbers are given in brackets. Together they bring Sheffield's past closer, by threading particular places into a simple narrative cloth.

From this evidence, the 'what' of the past, I have endeavoured to interpret, or give a 'how' and a 'why'. You may not agree with each of my conclusions, as Sheffield forges strong opinions. However, I hope you enjoy the book, the city, and each encourages you to find out and understand more.

CHAPTER ONE

The Place

'The town is about a mile in length, and half a mile in breadth; but the streets are narrow, and most of the houses appear black from the great clouds of smoak constantly issuing from the forges.'

The Modern Universal British Traveller 1779

'It were reet mucky, but now they've cleaned it up.'

Anon, 1992

To strangers, Sheffield = Steel. This simplification lies midway between a half-truth and a myth. Why is it still believed? Sometimes clung on to? How did it arise? In other words, what is the story behind the myth?

History is the setting and answering of questions about the past. Some cities, like York or Edinburgh, present a thesis better than others. A stranger seeing Sheffield today will find the past and present a jigsaw where the pieces don't quite seem to fit.

Leaving the M1 at Junction 33, the A630 dual-carriageway is unexceptional until it suddenly dips, a mile from the city centre. Sheffield rushes into view. To the left and south are Hyde Park and Park Hill high-rise flats dating from the sixties, already half-demolished, half-refurbished. Straight ahead, Park Square roundabout, icon to the motorcar, is congested with worshippers. To the right and north, the canal basin, a derelict reminder of the steel age, dark and brooding brick buildings awaiting redevelopment. Above your head the stanchions of Supertram, which will swoop and soar into the city, echoing the old tram system ditched just thirty years ago.

Two aspects stand out. Size: this picture of Sheffield shows development at an extreme of human scale; it defies immediate reconciliation with back-to-backs or individual ownership. Time: little more than a generation is recognized; it requires a stare to see the nineteenth century, and the more distant past is even harder to spot.

Exactly the same is true for the city centre. Odd pockets in an eighteenth-century garb (e.g. Paradise Square p. 52) survive. Before that, little more than a threadbare swatch of street patterns. The fact that

Four eras of transport from Park Hill Flats, looking north. At the centre Supertram grows out from the roundabout. Behind is the canal basin, opened in 1819, and awaiting redevelopment, with the viaduct of the defunct ex-Grand Central Railway at right angles. The present-day line runs within the cutting in the foreground

Sheffield was a thriving medieval town with its own massive castle has become difficult to imagine. It is simpler to believe Sheffield = Steel.

It is as simple as believing Sheffield lies at the centre of England. Open a road atlas in the middle and Sheffield will be there or thereabouts, and if all roads could be covered at equal speed, this would be true today. However, due to hills, rivers, climate and fundamental geology, the Sheffield area has always remained within a borderland, and far more isolated than a flat map projection indicates.

The Cambridge geographer Sir Cyril Fox first emphasized the importance of relief to overall UK settlement patterns during the 1920s. He divided the mainland into highland and lowland zones. Broadly speaking, the highlands run north-west of a line from Plymouth to Newcastle, to take in the Cornish Peninsula, the Quantocks, Wales, the Peak District, Pennines, North Yorks Moors, Cumbria and Lake District, the Cheviots and Scotland. It is a broad division, ignoring lowland areas like Cheshire, and south-east high-

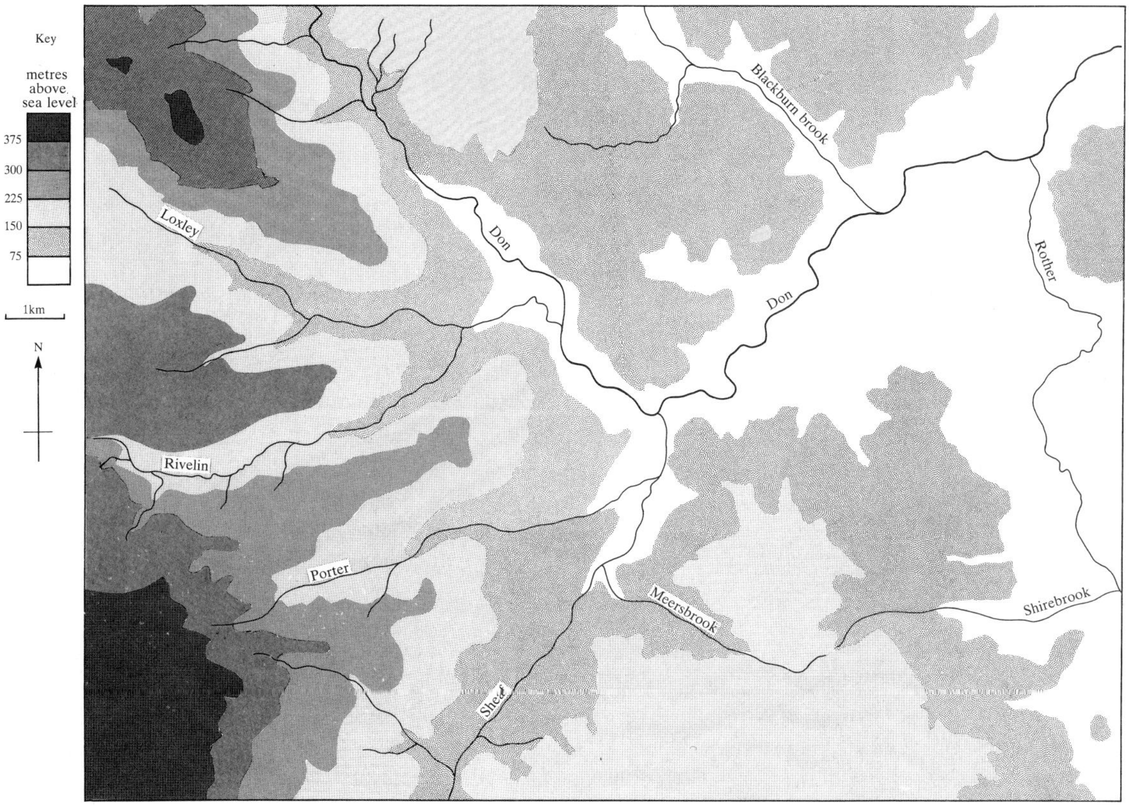

Sheffield area: relief and rivers

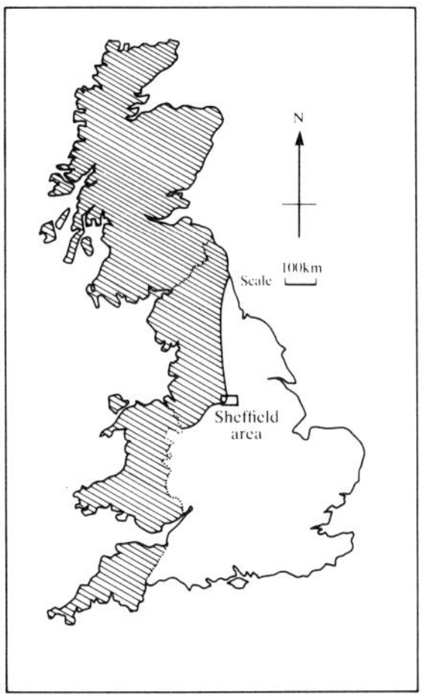

The Sheffield area, and the highland/lowland division

lands such as the South Downs. However, Sheffield is the only major city to lie astride this division. To the west of the rivers Don and Sheaf are hills, to their east are plains. Even down to TV regions, this is frontier country.

The map above shows how hillsides and river valleys shape Sheffield, which lies at the confluence of the Don and the Sheaf. The Lower Don Valley itself is the single flat route to the area. All other approaches require treks up and down hills. East of the Don and Sheaf these slopes are not too steep to deny straight roads which cut across contours, but to the west inclines graduate from the rugged to spectacular, as roads hug river valleys or twist themselves across harshly scarped slopes.

Sheffield is a city pushed up against the Derbyshire Peaks. A drive across any of the Pennine routes to Manchester will show that to you. It is still twisty, and in bad weather dangerous or impassable: think of that journey if your charge were a pack-horse team. There was no AA in the seventeeth century, but there were foot-pads and bandits.

More accessible to the east, roads largely failed to single out Sheffield before the planning and construction of the M1. Since prehistoric times the more direct north–south route has crossed the Don near Doncaster, a point not lost on Roman road or Victorian rail engineers. Less apparent today is the fact that Doncaster was the closest natural inland port to Sheffield. Before 1732, when the Don was rendered navigable to Tinsley, five miles downriver from Sheffield, all heavy goods had to travel by cart or wagon across unkempt highways – 'Execrably bad, very stony, and excessively full of holes,' as Arthur Young described the road to Rotherham in 1769. Add the cost of overnight accommodation and stabling, and it becomes clear how economically isolated – or sheltered – Sheffield remained until the eighteenth century.

'Denudation has invested the Sheffield country with a topography . . . expressive of the control of rocks over scenery.' Outcrop and Victorian housing, Psalter Lane

Geology isolated Sheffield, yet it provided easily grasped industrial opportunities. The exposed coal measures also contain iron ores, so it is again simple to say dig a shallow scoop, put a light to the coal and iron, and Sheffield = Steel. Too simple. It ignores both the qualities of the parent rock and the skills required to turn stone into metal. In fact seldom was local iron ore used commercially to make steel – it just wasn't good enough, yet in medieval times coal was regularly slung aside as waste in mining for iron. Charcoal was used instead to smelt, and here the abundant forests between the Pennine moorlands and east midland plains were assiduously managed.

Two other sources not present in the finished article, be it a penknife blade or a 'Supergun' barrel, were also readily available within the coal measures. First, fine-quality clays necessary for refractory linings were increasingly exploited from the late sixteenth century as forge and furnace were melded together. Benjamin Huntsman's development of crucible steel manufacture during the 1740s would have been impossible without the clays and the expertise to make crucibles resist temperatures of 1600°C: a hot kitchen oven is 200°C.

Second, the various grades of sandstone outcrops were ideal to put and finish an edge to a blade. Their generally strong structure allowed their use as grinding wheels as well as static stones. Although impurities rarely led to a wheel literally exploding in the grinder's face, the abraded dust would remorselessly clog his lungs, leading to *Silicosis*, slow internal drowning in dust.

The millstone grits were only suitable for flour mills and Peak National Park boundary stones. But their interplay with the coal measures results in eyebrow-raising ridges where uncounted streams clip down their slopes like the veins on a trailbiker's calf. These streams, fast and small, provide a simple form of energy to power mills, not for grinding grain but blades, starting in the fifteenth century.

Simplified sketch-map of general geology in Sheffield region

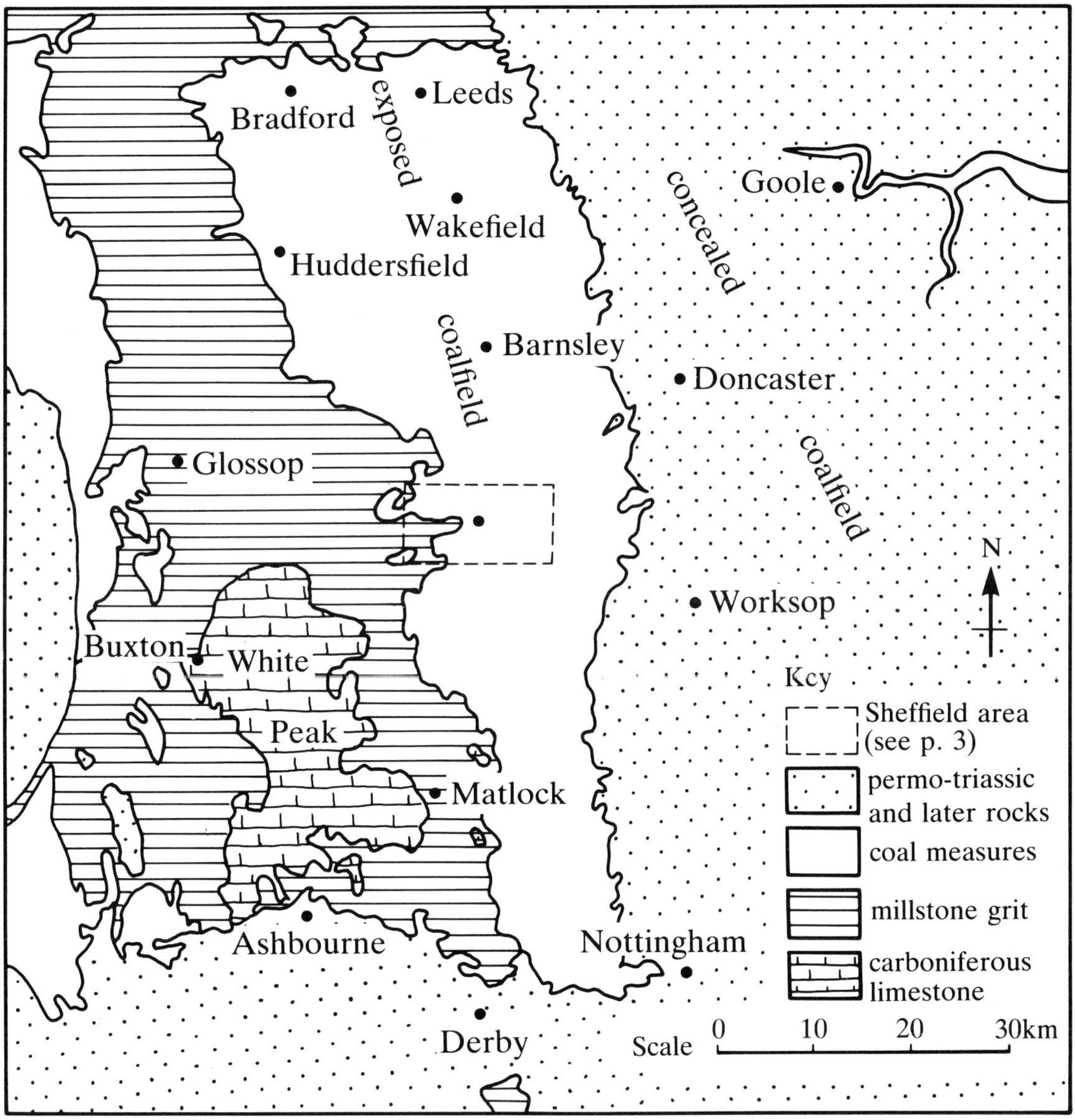
Bradford
Leeds
exposed
Wakefield
Huddersfield
coalfield
Barnsley
Goole
concealed
Doncaster
coalfield
Glossop
Worksop
N
Buxton
White
Peak
Matlock
Ashbourne
Nottingham
Derby
Kcy
Sheffield area
(see p. 3)
permo-triassic
and later rocks
coal measures
millstone grit
carboniferous
limestone
Scale
0
10
20
30km

None of these six natural attributes – coal, iron ore, refractory clays, grinding stones, woodlands and water power – are unique to the Sheffield area. The fact that they are linked together is. For example, the Forest of Dean lacked the clays and grinding stones, and despite the proximity of the ports of Bristol and Gloucester and a tradition reaching back to Roman times, its iron industry died as Sheffield's flourished. These six natural attributes define the initial conditions for Sheffield steel manufacture. They are necessary, but not sufficient.

'Nose to the grindstone.' Worn-out grindstones reused at Abbeydale Hamlet as a roof support. Water-powered bellows are to the right

Time and again we will see the preconditions for change in Sheffield defined, or put into place as it were, followed by a space or pause before they are taken up. As gaps these pauses may be viewed as a symptom of isolation. Nonetheless these hiatuses are vital since they indicate that change is not predetermined by material conditions, but influenced and effected by people, not rocks.

All six local attributes are now entering the past. Water wheels, charcoal coppicing, grindstones and iron adits have long been museum pieces, valued now only as heritage; coal is unlikely to last another generation, and of these original preconditions only refractory clays appear to possess a secure future in manufacture. The passing of these processes into history may evoke nostalgia but ought not to lead to dismay. Sheffield is again in a period of hiatus as it moves in the 1990s away from a solely manufacturing economy. Alongside this a seventh, less directly physical, attribute is diminishing, and that is the legacy of Sheffield's geographical isolation.

This has been a spur as much as a hindrance, a problem which provided opportunity. For example, it is easier to distribute small labour-intensive high quality products such as tools and cutlery by pack-horse or cart than equivalently priced bulkier commodities. In the economics of manufacture, Sheffield's central isolation has placed a premium upon quality, for which its workers may be rightfully proud.

Beyond economics, this interplay between borderland and seclusion becomes more intriguing. Their juxtaposition works from local to national levels, providing a heterogeneity which makes Sheffield Sheffield, and Sheffield interesting. At a local level the criss-crossing steepness of hillsides not only influenced the origin of settlements but has helped to maintain their particular identity and character. Names like Hillsborough, Crookes and Walkley aren't just entries in an A to Z, suburbs which merge like the shape of modern cars into one another; they are still sharply individual communities with their own style and ways of doing things. This led to Sheffield being named the largest village in England, a title now difficult to reconcile with 1991 Meadowhall, the largest shopping centre in Europe – just as in the same way thatched cottage commutervilles estrange themselves from traditional rural attitudes.

In Sheffield these village values survive strongest in how the city is laid out, and how people regard others. The city doesn't sprawl; it comprises a field of houses here, a field of offices there, a field of shops, a field of factories, a field of parks and a field of wasteland. The pattern is parochial, nearly disjointed, and it isn't simply a matter of adapting to hills. Edinburgh, Bath, Bristol and nearby Buxton are all towns with distinctive topography yet each possesses an urban layout. Strangers to Sheffield find this puzzling. Every aspect of urban life – cinemas, breweries, clubs, libraries, museums, showrooms – is present, but not fitted together from the centre. It is neither planned nor organic but a mixture of the two.

Of course, people who live or work in Sheffield are so used to this that they in turn are puzzled by strangers finding the layout not at all straightforward. Why shouldn't a little old cutlery factory building sit beside a modern office block?

Being a Sheffielder means membership of a complex cultural value system which arises directly from the city's physical structure. For example, coming from Netheredge on the west side of the Sheaf is altogether distinct from Heeley, on the other bank of a river you can now scarcely see. Add to this ethnic, religious, gender and age groupings, not to mention class, and from a village Sheffield becomes an eclectic jamboree, honestly celebrated in myriad local stories, histories and legends, now perhaps coming together at the start of each summer during the Sheffield Festival.

Differences do occur. Sheffield people are quick to blame Sheffield people in the privacy of their own village-city: it's t'council's fault bus's late, while ex-union and management still lay into each other about the collapse of the heavy metal trade. Frontiers and isolation extend from settlement patterns, directly translated, into work places. One shop-branch or council department will privately flatter or besmirch another, as behind these scenes gossamer webs of chinese whispers coat the simplest transaction with delightful gossip. Here, this human commonplace is an addict's habit.

Yet to the outside world Sheffield will defend its own to the death. People are interested in outsiders who visit: while you use this book as a guide, friendly passers-by will help you too! However, they are less keen to display their own concerns to the outside world. Proud of their city, yet shy of going beyond it, this too is a characteristic of village life.

This strange one-way mirror reflects the city's greatest isolation. The Tiv in Nigeria used to measure distance in terms of kindred

closeness: neighbours may live miles away, strangers next door. The gap between Sheffield and Rotherham is far wider than the M1, and the city boundary, twice changed in living memory, is a moat unimaginable to the West Midlands, where only a ticket or road map is required to move from Wolverhampton to Coventry. The city's pride brings shelter and warmth to its isolation and independence.

Sheffield is on the edge and in between things. The largest city in Yorkshire, it lies at the foot of the county, little more than a stone's throw from Derbyshire or Nottinghamshire. Similarly it straddles the border between the midlands and the north. To a southerner it is the north, to a northerner it's on the way south. Sir Cyril Fox's highland and lowland division still survives from mesolithic hunter-gatherers 10,000 years ago. As a locus Sheffield is an island geographically central to the rest of the country.

The clearest survival of this is how people speak – one of the oldest things in the city. Within a week of coming to Sheffield in 1976 I heard a Radio Three programme discuss how ye Olde English way of pronouncing *-igh* had died out during the seventeenth century. No one in Sheffield or in the BBC had bothered listening to each other: in a pub that night, people pronounced 'night' to rhyme with 'kicked' rather than 'kite', just as they did in the 1600s. This way of speaking is on the wane. Today's visitor may be told that Sheffield is like Rome, a city of seven hills. I doubt whether a Caesar, Cicero or Pavarotti would make the connection. Rome is the eternal city, Sheffield a city of change, eternal change, and that is its historical attraction and charm.

A minute's walk from the city centre. On the left the rear of the NUM National Headquarters, on the right the Sheffield Rubber Stamp Company. In between, a long narrow street, Carver Lane, typifies pre-Victorian Sheffield

CHAPTER TWO

Origins

According to the archaeological record people first came to the Sheffield area about 45,000 years ago. How do we know that? Evidence is scarce and hard to come by: only what is buried, dug up and recorded. As unwitting time capsules, people left stone and bone artefacts at caves we now call Cresswell Crags, twenty miles south-west of the Sheaf/Don confluence, for archaeologists to recover this century.

Forty-five thousand years is an enormous gap of time. If each word in this sentence were a single year, 45,000 years is almost twice the length of this entire book. We call these people Neanderthals, and though their lifestyles are almost unrecognizable to us, anatomically we and they are judged the same species, any difference being racial. Given this gap, and its smattering of remains, the picture archaeologists have constructed is remarkably good, and the site is well worth visiting for itself and its interpretation (See p. 117).

Temperatures dropped as the ice-caps grew, and the caves were deserted until about 30,000 years ago. The caves were also dens to hyenas, bears and other predators, with humans the less frequent visitors. Outside the caves the environment, particularly the fauna, was very different. As well as hyenas and bears, now-extinct species such as bison, giant reindeer and woolly rhinos roamed. Perhaps these people survived by trapping animals as they trekked through the gorge of the caves, contributing to their extinction.

As nomadic hunters they trekked too, hundreds of miles, if comparisons with recent hunters can be patterned into the past. They shouldn't just be seen as cave-people as they would have lived on many other sites, it's just that the caves best protect evidence. They could have hunted up into glaciers at the foot of the Peaks, and across to Denmark and north Germany. The North Sea was dry land then.

These people left the caves to other predators for 12–15,000 years, although we cannot be sure they entirely abandoned the area. The next spate of evidence is more specialized: stone tools with a greater degree of selection in material, design and manufacture, chosen hunting of wild horse judging by the bone remnants, decorated artefacts, and the deliberate burial of their dead. Here is a group we can more easily identify with.

From a bolt-hole between glaciers, Creswell Crags had probably become just one of a seasonal suite of sites as the migratory habits steadily grew more regular. With the end of the ice-age, around 11,000 years ago, we start to see a spread of activity and sites across the landscape. Archaeologically this typifies the change from the Upper Palaeolithic to the Mesolithic.

Excavations of three open sites straddle the area: on the Notts, Derbyshire, South Yorkshire intersection, Thorpe Common; between Sheffield and Chesterfield, Unstone; and to the north, on Wharncliffe Edge, Deepcar. Rescued in 1962 in advance of quarrying, this site highlights Sheffield's location upon the boundary of highland and lowland zones. Relatively large pieces of Lincolnshire flint were found, together with good evidence of stone foundations for some sort of shelter and windbreak, with hearths.

Working primarily from relative frequencies of buried pollen, the local climate and vegetation was more extreme then: long cold winters with short hot summers, broader expanses of forests and uplands. In order to move from habitat to habitat people needed to travel commensurately long distances, hence the Lincolnshire flint at Deepcar. The knapping of flint tools leaves behind scrap or debitage. Analysis of

Simplified excavation plan of Deepcar site

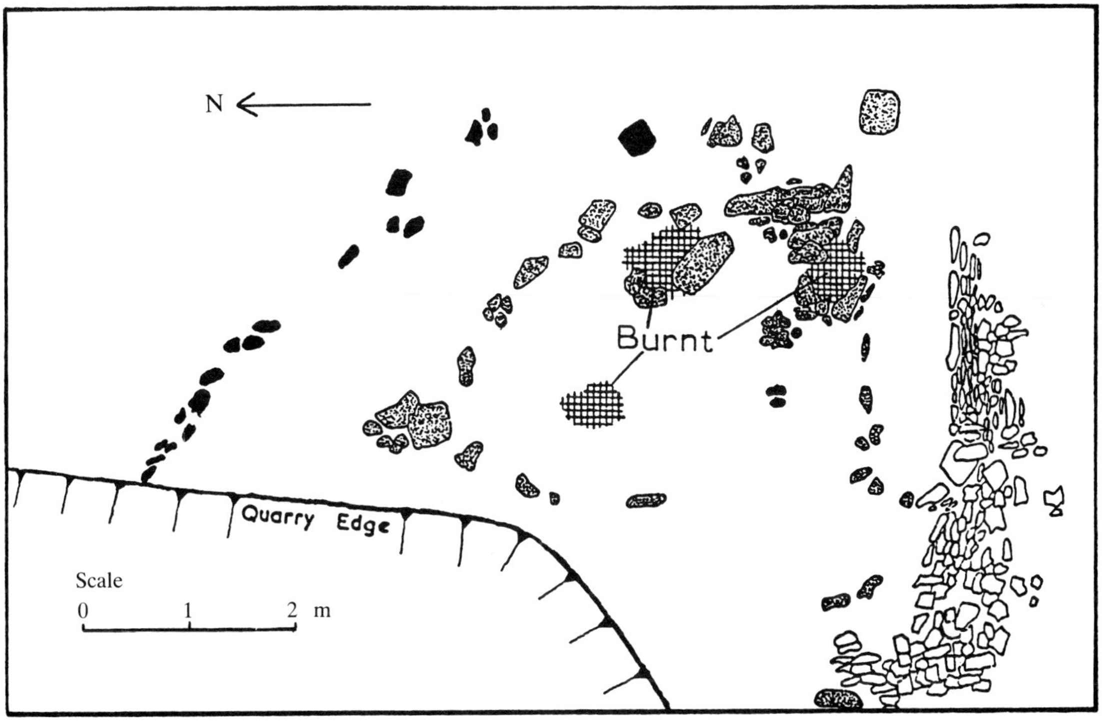

this prehistoric industry shows Deepcar was probably a base-camp for seasonal hunters preparing tools to follow deer-herds on to their summer upland grazing, and regularly returning in order to exploit the highlands from the more sheltered lowlands. If you look from Wharncliffe Side to Wharncliffe Wood across the Don between the city and Stocksbridge, you are staring at the first known area in the vicinity of Sheffield to be deliberately selected as a place to live.

Two thousand years later a more intricate pattern appears to emerge, together with a more varied pattern of vegetation and equitable climate. Unstone and Thorpe Common were more likely to be settlements rather than base-camps, supported by longer term strategies of forest burning to promote increased deer-herd sizes as well as plant resources such as hazel nuts. These fires were the first steps towards environmental degradation, creating today's 'natural' moorlands in the Peak District. Fishing took off and, as the North Sea grew, the first catch was probably hooked from Salmon Pastures in the Lower Don.

By 6,500 BC the Channel had separated Britain from Europe, and the focus of settlement had moved to the Peak area, in the west and south-west of the map on p. 13.

Here the local picture becomes rather vague due to a lack of evidence. Unlike documents, which only seem to pile up, archaeological sites tend to be buried or destroyed by later sites. The Peaks have not been built upon, which means both preservation and recovery ratios are higher. Having said that, it seems the Sheffield area was a relative backwater in the mesolithic/neolithic transition, when people developed ways of growing plants and rearing animals as well as hunting and gathering.

The fields and herds of these first farmers nevertheless extended into the area. A previous generation of archaeologists talked of a 'neolithic revolution' together with successive waves of invaders such as the 'Beaker People' of the Bronze Age. There is scant evidence for this. The change between mesolithic hunter-gatherers and neolithic farmers, though total, is also gradual, while the transference of designs and styles across the Channel indicates peace as much as war. With the Third Reich on the doorstep of a threatened empire, such an interpretation was understandable. The fact that today's National Curriculum, in its only mention of European prehistory, still speaks of a 'neolithic revolution' and ages of invaders, is hard to understand and harder to condone, since it compels schools to teach error as truth.

This is brought home by the map on p. 13. According to the evidence, the neolithic and Bronze Age shared similar sites. A visit to the City Museum's Human History gallery (p. 117) will show you that

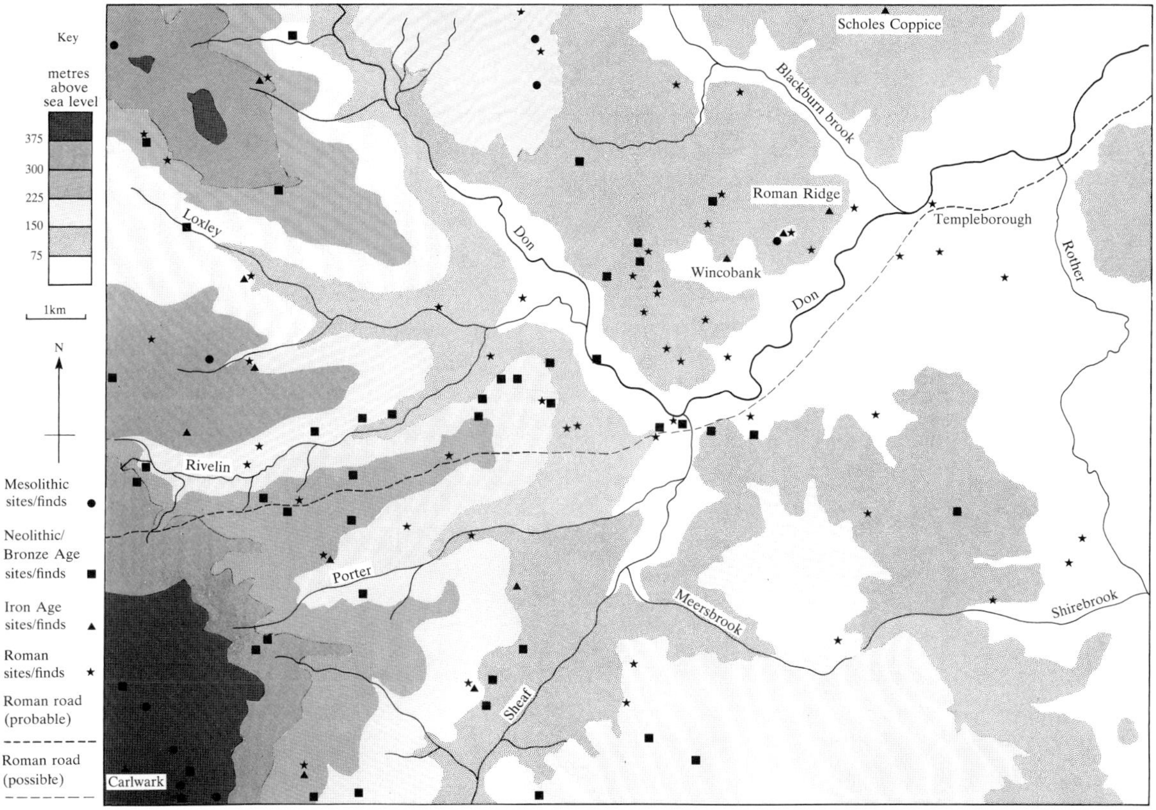

Sheffield area finds and sites: mesolithic, neolithic and Bronze Age, Iron Age, Roman

although styles of pottery, flint and metalwork alter, they do so progressively, quite unlike the difference between native Iron Age and incoming Roman material.

Farming enabled and enforced a change from a nomadic to a sedentary life. The White Peak is the first and arguably the richest neolithic area within the region, and its initial position is mirrored by similar settlement patterns on the magnesium limestone of the Lincolnshire wolds to the east. It is only in the later neolithic period, between 3,500 and 2,000 BC, that settlement spreads across the Dark Peak and its millstone grits into the Sheffield area. The map above shows this trend, where virtually all the material is located on the Grit uplands to the west, as opposed to the coal measures to the east. This could, of course, be an accident of collection, just as the pre-war clump of prehistoric sites around Oxford was related to the distance undergraduate members of the University Archaeological Society were happy to bicycle in a day, but since much of the eastern area was a medieval hunting park surviving in part into the nineteenth century, if there were sites and finds to be found, they would have been.

This again emphasizes Sheffield's position on the border between highland and lowland Britain. Here the area was peripheral to the massive monuments such as Arbor Low, just off the A515 midway between Buxton and Ashbourne, or long barrows like Duggleby Howe in Lincolnshire. However, at Ash Cabin Flat a small stone circle just about survives, more or less similar to those in the Peak District, such as near Robin Hood's Stride on Harthill Moor, in the centre of the White Peak. Especially as it is now far harder to touch Stonehenge than at any time since it was built, Robin Hood's Stride and Arbor Low are both worth seeing in order to appreciate the social energy, organization and purpose necessary to construct these monuments, over and above the demands of everyday life. Each is as politically complex as Sheffield Arena, Don Valley Stadium or Ponds Forge Baths.

Ash Cabin Flat looks across to Lodge Moor Hospital, once a site of Bronze Age round barrows. It is curious that neolithic henges and long barrows were succeeded by smaller and more numerous round barrows during the Bronze Age, and most archaeologists agree this reflects, through death, burial and grave-goods, society's formal recognition of individual status.

Exactly who was recognized will never be known, but the Rivelin valley seems a local focus for neolithic and Bronze Age settlement, successively moving from the millstone grits on to the sandstone rises of the coal measures. Fields were made by moving aside stones, and evidence of this still survives in the Bronze Age clearance cairns – low stone clumps usually driven past today, without a second glance to the fields beyond the Toad's Mouth on the A625, below the brooding, enigmatic and undated Carlwark.

These fields were small, hand-cultivated, and more akin to allotments. Grinding stones for flour-milling were quarried from outcrops, notably by Carlwark and Wharncliffe. These were also powered by hand rather than wind, water or animal, and there is a fine display of them at the City Museum. Meat, milk and grain were probably augmented by fish and wildfowl, given the 7 ft long dug-out canoe found in the Don's silts in 1963 and radiocarbon dated to 1500 BC.

How the Toad's Mouth fields fell out of cultivation is not known, but there is no real evidence beyond the Iron Age, so it is quite possible this farming led directly to the soil degradation that characterizes the moorland today.

A low and heather-clad Bronze Age clearance cairn: a relic of field-making three to four thousand years ago above Toad's Mouth near Foxhouse

Environmental destruction goes back thousands of years, to the forest burning during the mesolithic. Its effects were just as sure as Amazonian rain forest burning today, yet since Wordsworth the myth of untrammelled nature has promulgated itself even into planning statutes. How many of us feel the Peak District is as God created? The countryside left behind is not nature untouched by human hand but a landscape entirely created by generation after generation for thousands of years. That is its attraction.

Why didn't people cultivate the coal measures during the neolithic and Bronze Age? Try digging a garden on their clays and you have your answer: it is hard work requiring drainage as well as muscle. The map on p. 13 shows the spread of Iron Age remains. The lack of finds is largely due to a switch from stone-edged to metal-edged tools, where the metal was either recycled and/or corroded away following discard. Pottery, the prehistorians' other staple, is rarely tough enough to survive frost and ploughing after casual discard.

Yet again we see a west/east, highland/lowland division along the Don/Sheaf valleys. The sites themselves reflect political territories: hillforts to control hill and vale. Prime among these is Wincobank. The only hillfort in Europe inside city limits, its builders from its ramparts in the sixth century BC would have seen the Don winding between woodlands, pasture and arable fields – a picture which would scarcely change overall for over 2,000 years.

A glance north-east would have found Scholes Coppice, a much smaller defended site, whose occupiers were potential allies, outposts or enemies of Wincobank.

Aerial photo of Wincobank hillfort from the east. The double ring earthworks would have protected houses, which now flank either side of the promontory

The earth piled high from the small excavation trench of the small enclosure demonstrates how much more would have to have been hewn and transported by hand in order to build Wincobank. Each of these sites is a product, symbol and control of political power as much as the Town Hall and steel works to follow in the valley below.

With similar double bank, ditches and radiocarbon dates, Wincobank is grouped with Mam Tor, or 'the shivering mountain' and tourist trap above Castleton in the Peaks. Carlwark, overlooking the A625 at Foxhouse, is more enigmatic, with suggested dates ranging from late neolithic to early Saxon. Equally, it seems certain that the linear earthwork immediately north-east of Wincobank called Roman Ridge is not Roman. It may be Saxon, a remnant of a minor version of Offa's Dyke (which Mercia's King Offa had built to divide his kingdom from Celtic Wales); or it may be Iron Age, similar to linear earthworks in the lowland zone that demarcated territories during the final two centuries BC. It may even be both! This nebulous chronology is only partially caused by a lack of dating evidence. Just as Sheffield Cathedral and market have been religious and retail sites for a thousand years, neolithic henges, Bronze Age barrows and Iron Age hill-

Plan and photo of Scholes Coppice excavation. Contrast with Templeborough, with which it may have co-existed

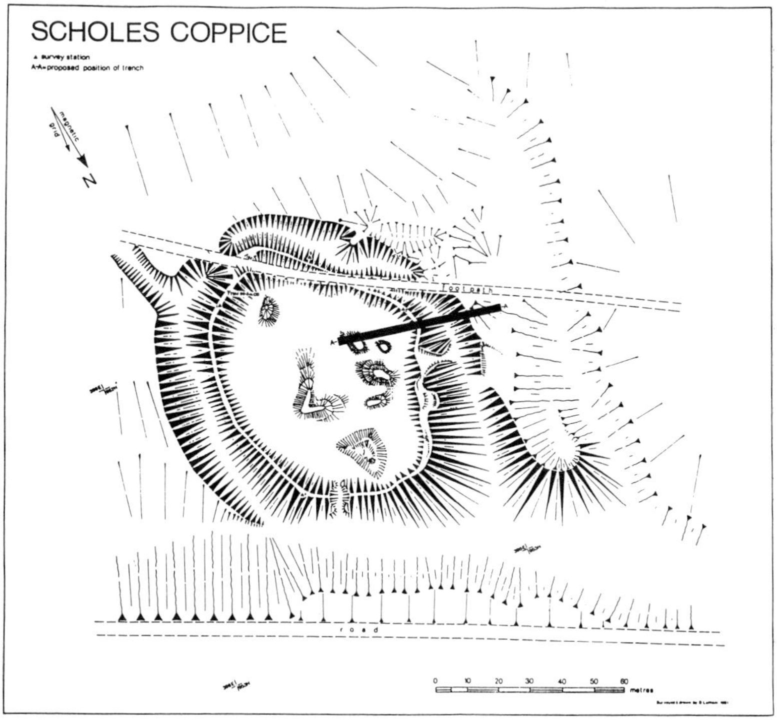

forts can also have long lives. Uncertainties aside, Wincobank and its peers were built to defend and protect – but what?

On the less built-up millstone grits, more recent stone dykes preserve or cut across earlier fields of farming systems which straddle the Iron Age and Roman periods. Here is the fossilized economy which not only must have extended across today's built-up area and produced enough to feed the farmers and the hillfort builders, but also by the time the Romans first invaded in 55 BC, was exporting grain, something which has never been achieved since.

We know this through Roman commentators. At this interface between prehistory and history they also gave us the first names of people to place along the highland/lowland division. Brigantes is the Latin-transcribed Celtic name for the people who built these sites, the Coritanni being those east of the lower Don. Beyond this it becomes more difficult to ascribe exact boundaries or relationships. One may draw maps and pictures of Celtic chiefdoms and chiefs, but at this distance it is akin to watching the progress of a foreign civil war on TV with the sound turned down. What stands proud is how the Sheffield area continues to lie upon a border. The landscape now gains a political commentary.

The heavier clay and alluvial soils east of the millstone grits were probably ploughed before Roman occupation. They certainly were under *Pax Britannia*. Templeborough is the only Imperial site in the area. As the map on p. 13 shows, it lies on the south bank of the Don overlooked by Wincobank. It was originally a fort but later developed stone buildings, with bath-houses and an industrial estate between its walls and the Don. Perhaps the river was then navigable, if only seasonally, upstream from Doncaster?

Buried beneath the British Steel Corporation, the Romans were first to smelt iron and exploit coal – to manufacture glass. This seemed to cover local needs without the planned colonial trading structure imposed to export lead from Derbyshire adits. Agriculture developed to exploit the heavier coal measure soils, which meant iron-shared ploughs and wintering-over of plough-teams. This may sound simple, but it was the onset of mechanization. Rotherham's Clifton Park Museum (p. 117) as well as displaying Templeborough material, has reconstructed the remains of a specialized corn-drying building, part of a production line of factory farming – very different to the Bronze Age fields at Toad's Mouth.

Templeborough was not the routeway centre that *Danum* (Doncaster), a vast civilian settlement surrounding the military walls, became. Rather it was a staging post, the last lowland site on the road

Templeborough Roman Fort. Original 1916–17 excavation plans

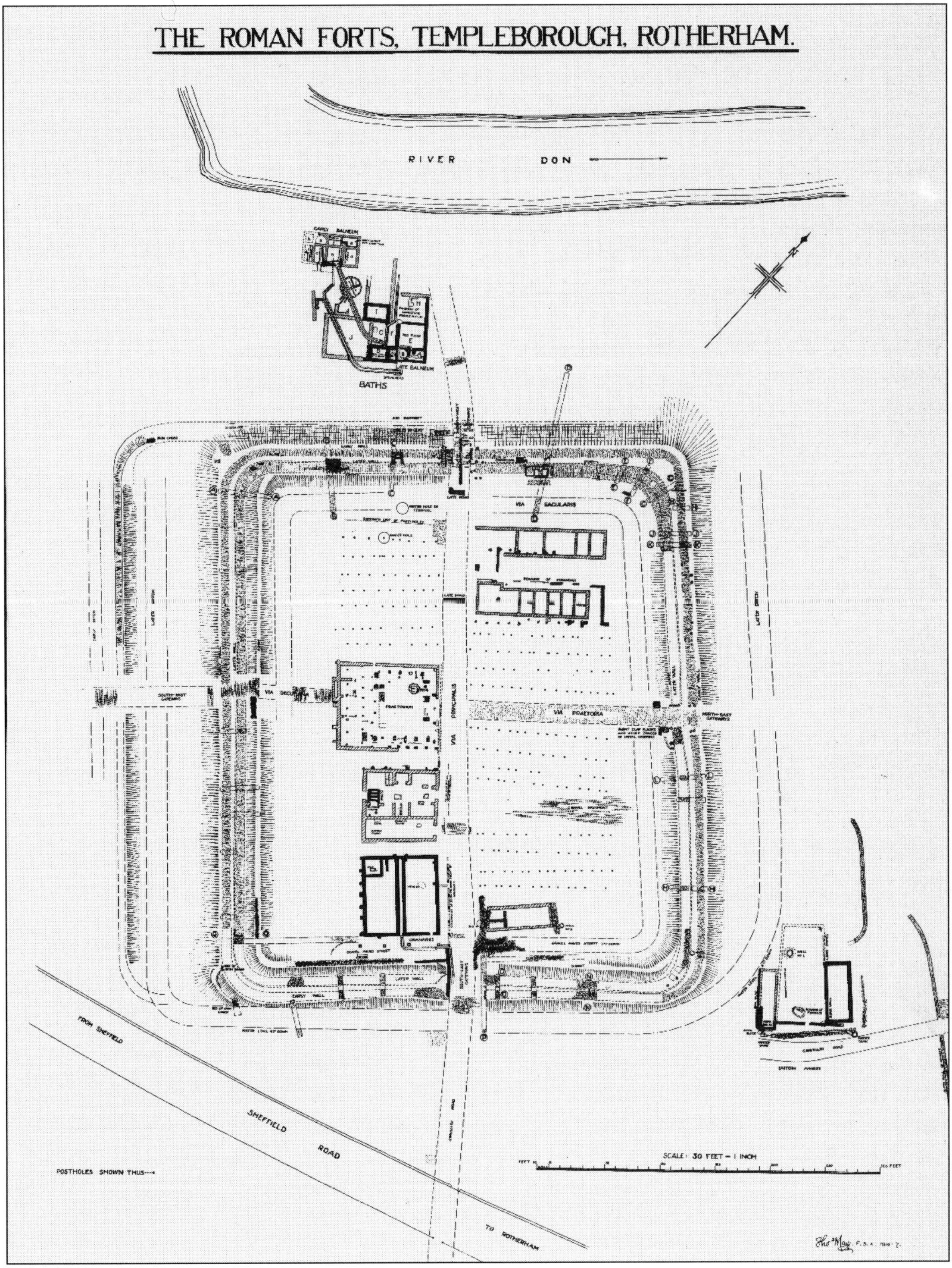
THE ROMAN FORTS, TEMPLEBOROUGH, ROTHERHAM.
RIVER DON
BATHS
VIA SAGULARIS
VIA PRINCIPALIS
VIA PRAETORIA
PRAETORIUM
GRANARIES
FROM SHEFFIELD
SHEFFIELD ROAD
TO ROTHERHAM
SCALE: 30 FEET = 1 INCH
POSTHOLES SHOWN THUS

to Chester, which undoubtedly went via Brough, near Hope, and Buxton, but whose line within Sheffield is not as clearcut as some authors like to make out. Not one piece of metalling or frontage has yet been excavated. Some proposed lines are later routes, some may well be earlier.

As interesting is the distribution of coins and coin hoards. Money, the stuff Marx brilliantly defined as the commodity which buys commodities, was known in Celtic Europe but the Romans developed its universality. From Perth to Persia their coinage was recognized, clipped and forged, a hard ECU 2,000 years ahead of its time. In the Sheffield area, the map on p. 13 shows how native or Romano-British life shared this economy, and the concentration of coins on the higher grounds to the west indicates these remained the more developed or wealthier parts. Focusing this picture, the distribution pattern within the parishes of Bradfield, Sheffield and Ecclesfield maps out in such a way as to imply that the fundamental Saxon and later political landscape already existed in embryo.

CHAPTER THREE

A Village in Hallamshire

Whatever the antonym for '*veni, vidi, vici*', the Roman galleys finally left Britain with rather less gung-ho than their first landing over four centuries earlier. For local historian and archaeologist there follows a two century dearth of evidence before the recognition of Anglo-Saxon settlements. During this period the Sheffield area came under the British kingdom of Elmet which survived being sandwiched between the Anglo-Saxon kingdoms of Mercia and Northumbria until the early seventh century. Or rather, it remained a secluded geographical pocket or border region which lay out of the way of increasingly powerful political forces.

Place-name evidence fits this thesis. Only the *-ham* of Rotherham is early Anglo-Saxon, and here the newcomers picked out the old Celtic river name. Likewise Ecclesall and Ecclesfield perpetuate the British name for church. Both the native Britons and incoming Saxons, if not all Christians, at least respected the Church. In comparison with the old empire days of Rome, there certainly was a decline in organized trade, industry and civic life, but no wholesale devastation. Angles and Saxons were as much migrants as invaders; their bad press as bloodthirsty foreigners resulted from their lack of control of the media as much as objective fact.

Nor should we assume entirely Anglo-Saxon names imply entirely Anglo-Saxon settlements. Names but not the places may change; for example, Windscale reverting back to Sellafield in 1981. Clumps of Mercians, Northumbrians and Britons lived together in what had become a borderland, where political boundaries were altered by acts of sword rather than acts of parliament. After the Battle of Hatfield in 633, King Penda of Mercia ruled up to Airedale until 654, when he died in battle, and Yorkshire reverted to Northumbria once more. You can imagine a Sheffield couple discussing the news: 'Dost thee know, love, we're Northumbrian again.'

'No, just while I was getting used to those mild Mercian winters.'

With the Anglo-Saxon world of England overtaking the old British land of Albion, the name of Sheffield is first registered. It is no accident nor coincidence that the *sheaf* part means boundary: this naming of both river and settlement is the first mapping of an increasingly political division born from its geography.

As David Hey points out (see p. 117), Sheffield, Ecclesfield and Bradfield become loci within their landscapes. Evidence such as the Roman coin-concentrations from the previous chapter, the church at Ecclesfield, and the early antiquity of Dronfield and Chesterfield immediately to the south in north Derbyshire all indicate that these places build upon pre-existing settlement patterns and practices.

Sheffield is a modern industrial city, engulfing Ecclesfield by suburban growth. Just Bradfield, on its moor, remains a village, with a flavour of its Saxon history readily apparent to a visitor. Each place is also characterized by a Saxon Christian cross, the only ones to survive within the area.

The Sheffield Cross has an interesting history. Erected in the tenth century, it was removed in 1570 from its original location in the precincts of the present-day cathedral, only to be rediscovered in a cutler's workshop in Victorian times employed, with one side grooved out, as a hardening trough. This says something about how different epochs have viewed the value of historical objects in Sheffield. It displays a fine set of motifs and styles which means it has a national significance, and therefore has been moved to the British Museum, London. Unlike Melina Mercouri as Greek Minister of Culture demanding the return of the Elgin Marbles to Greece, no one from Sheffield has petitioned the BM for the Cross to return to where it started from.

Whether or not each cross stood alone or, as they did later, with a church building, they would have served as a centre for local gossip and administration as well as worship. *Hallam* meant rock or stone, and the parishes of Sheffield, Bradfield and Ecclesfield combined together to form Hallamshire.

This is the greatest legacy from pre-conquest England. It existed as a local 'mental' map long after it lost its medieval shire status, administrative clout and national recognition. As Defoe wrote in the 1720s: '. . . in Derbyshire, wrought iron and edge-tools, of all sorts, from the forges at Sheffield, and from the country call'd Hallamshire . . .' Derbyshire and Sheffield need no explanation by Defoe to his reader, whereas Hallamshire, a local term, does. Today it survives not so much as a geographical entity, but more a coda of finery to gentrify Sheffield names: no Sheffield hospital bears Sheffield in its title, but

The Sheffield Cross. A copy on display in Sheffield City Museum

Hallamshire, as laid down in Saxon times

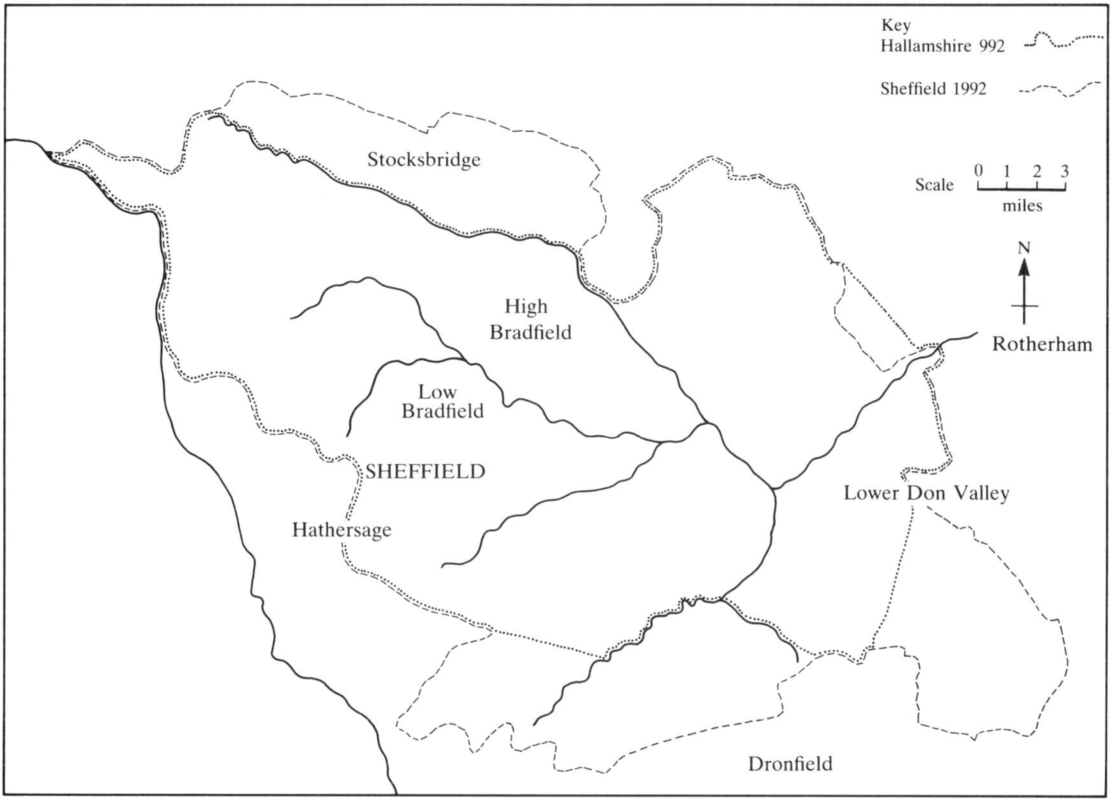

the most recent and most prestigious proclaims itself The Royal Hallamshire. 1992 sees the City Polytechnic renamed Sheffield Hallam University, although one of its sites, Totley, never lay within Hallamshire.

The exact boundaries of Hallamshire are hard to locate now, and perhaps always were; their original definition was the more important. A rough approximation today is between Junctions 33 to 35 on the M1 and the Derwent and Ladybower reservoirs in the Peak District, which shows how vast are the changes to a historical landscape, yet how it can still be perceived. Working back from the earliest medieval records, local historians all agree that as with its parishes, rivers and streams formed the basis of its perimeter. The gaps in between are the cause of uncertainty.

The southern boundary appears to have been the politically more sensitive and circumscribed. *Sheaf* means boundary, while *Meersbrook* means brook of the boundary – this was also the southern frontier of Northumbria. Similarly at Whirlow, Ringinglow and Stanage Pole, pre-existing features seem to be used, perhaps enhanced to make the border clear to locals and visitors alike. Today, thick-socked trekkers of the thirty-mile Round Sheffield walk heed Anglo-Saxon bootsteps and land divisions down the Limb Valley, from Ringinglow to Whirlow Bridge.

It is no coincidence that this was also the border between Mercia and Northumbria. Thus Egbert of Wessex, in his rise to be king of kings within the seven Anglo-Saxon kingdoms in 830, deliberately 'led a levy to Dore against the Northumbrians and they submitted to him and peace was declared'.

By 942 the *Anglo-Saxon Chronicle* can record that Edmund conquered the Danes of Mercia 'as where the Dore divides'. The writers of the *Chronicle* are not likely to have travelled this way, yet their words indicate how firmly fixed and narrow this boundary had become, separating Yorkshire from Derbyshire, and the diocese of York from Lichfield.

The survival of Hallamshire can now be judged as the conclusion of a border region. In the preceding chapter we saw how the Sheffield area before the Romans was a political frontier between the Celtic Brigantes and Coritanni. This pattern continued after the Romans left, with the British kingdom of Elmet being squeezed down to 'where the Dore divides'. Hallamshire continued to be a borderland in the more hotch-potch political geography associated with the Danes, and the reaction of the country and William the Conquerer to each other. Bearing in mind that even today Sheffield and the remainder of

Stone at Dore to commemorate peace in their time

KING ECGBERT OF WESSEX
LED HIS ARMY TO DORE
IN THE YEAR A·D 829
AGAINST KING EANRED
OF NORTHUMBRIA
BY WHOSE
SUBMISSION
KING ECGBERT
BECAME FIRST
OVERLORD
OF ALL
ENGLAND

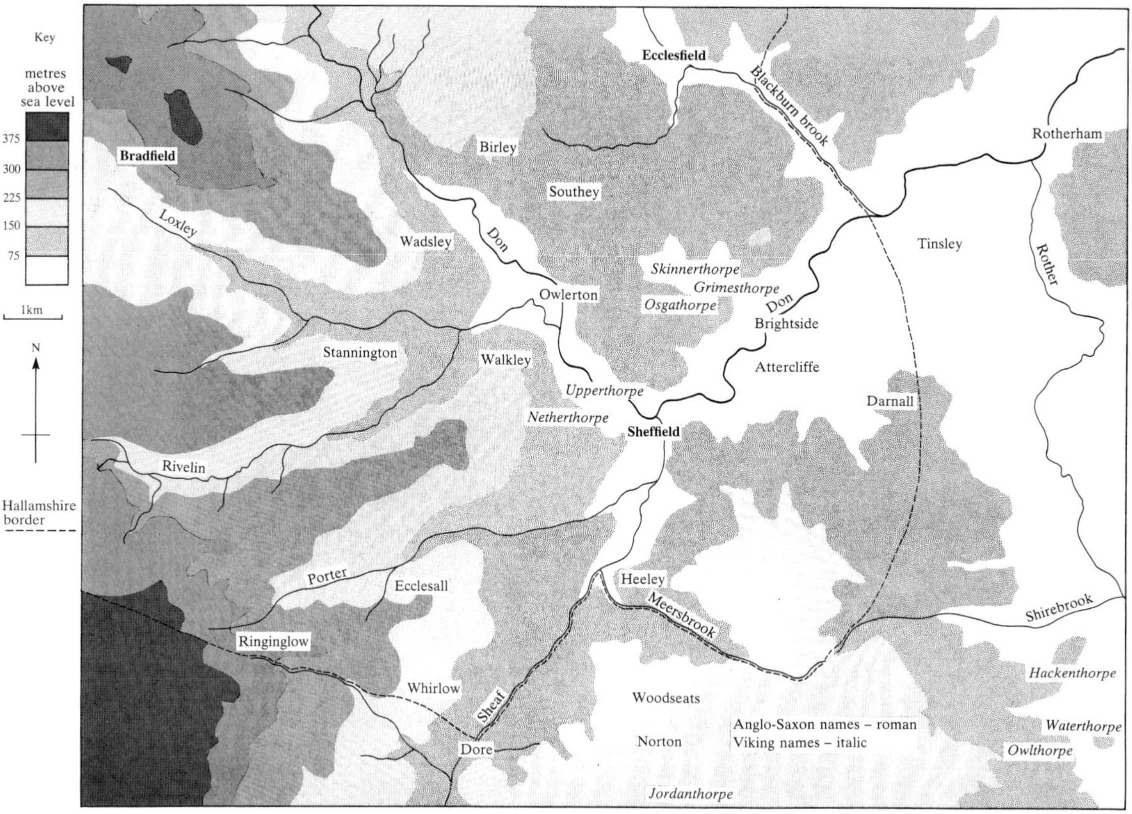

Place-names before 1066

Yorkshire often perceive themselves as dissimilar entities, it may be asked not why Hallamshire survives for so long, but how the Sheffield area has not maintained a more enduring political sovereignty.

Politics aside, by the time Danish settlements appear in the records, the majority of local place-names are established. We should not think places like Attercliffe or Heeley were originally cosy rural villages, regardless of what they are today. They were by the end of the Middle Ages, but that was over five hundred years into the future; closer in time to now than then. Dispersed hamlets would be a more apt term, a group of farms attached to a common path or spring, something akin to the grouping of houses at Ringinglow or Wharncliffe Side today.

The Danish settlements – characterized by *-thorpe* or 'small farmstead' suffixes – would have fitted into this pattern. It is intriguing to see how they cluster tightly together and largely to the east. It is likely they were taking in the poorer quality sites not already under full cultivation, with the easier worked soils to the west having less space for new settlements. Neighbours will have differences, and at times of war these would have been exacerbated. However, from place-name evidence alone there is no reason to believe that Danes and Anglo-Saxons in the Sheffield area were at each others' throats. Also the recorded battles are either to the north or south. A more likely scenario is that their kings organized the fighting while their subjects looked out for themselves, and made allegiances and arrangements upon that basis. Thus Ecclesall and Brightside each came to be appended with 'bierlow', a Viking term of land administration, which did not die out until the nineteenth century.

More intriguing is the settlement 'flat spot' on the map bounded by Sheffield, Heeley, Darnall and the thorpes beside Hackenthorpe. After the Norman conquest this was to become a great hunting park, the land of the lord of the manor. This may well have been established in custom by or during the eleventh century, together with the communities within Hallamshire coming to the confluence of the Sheaf and Don to market produce. With the church, both the manor and the market survive today, and together they helped a village in Hallamshire develop into a town during the Middle Ages.

CHAPTER FOUR

A Cutting Edge

Duke William of Normandy conquered by sword, King William I consolidated by bureaucracy. The Domesday Book recorded the first detailed picture of life inside Hallamshire. Sheffield as 'Escafeld' is a lesser part within Hallam, which has led to a hunt for its pre-conquest manorial hall. There is no documentary, cartographical, archaeological or other evidence except for a large three-bayed Anglo-Saxon timber building excavated 1927–9 under Castle Market in the city centre.

Today the Don doesn't look a big river, while the Sheaf within the city centre runs entirely underground (apart from when it decides to flood the railway station as it did at Christmas 1991).Their confluence, however, provided both an excellent defensive site and meeting place. Incoming Normans were to be told that this was where manorial affairs were dealt with since 'time whereof the memory of men runneth not to the contrary'. Together with the Saxon stone cross we can draw a bare map of Sheffield in 1066.

The High Street today with its wild buffalo herds of buses and all too concrete Hole in the Road is hardly like its Victorian precursor, never mind Anglo-Saxon. But it is the street which the other medieval streets respect, and it may well have formed a route between the cross, hall and a crossing of the Sheaf – perhaps the same since Roman times. Such a transport interchange had come to be a market and focus for settlement within the fields.

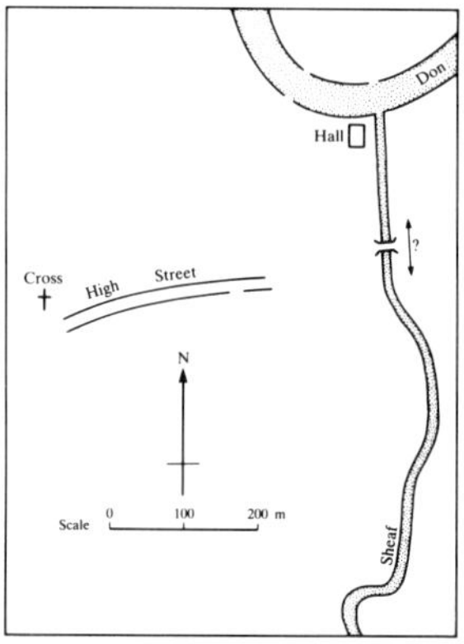

Sheffield, 1066

Owner-occupier of the hall was Waltheof, a native Northumbrian who switched political allegiances about as often as Dr David Owen, and with as much – or as little – success. William left him in possession after Hastings in 1066. In 1069 Waltheof rebelled with the northern lords, but made his peace after the rebellion failed, and in return William entrusted him with the Earldom of Huntingdon and the hand of his niece Judith. Waltheof conspired to rebel in 1075 and failed again, but this time William had him beheaded instead of just married into the family. His widow Judith inherited the lot (while Waltheof's memory is perpetuated by a school and sports centre bearing his name just off the A630 Parkway).

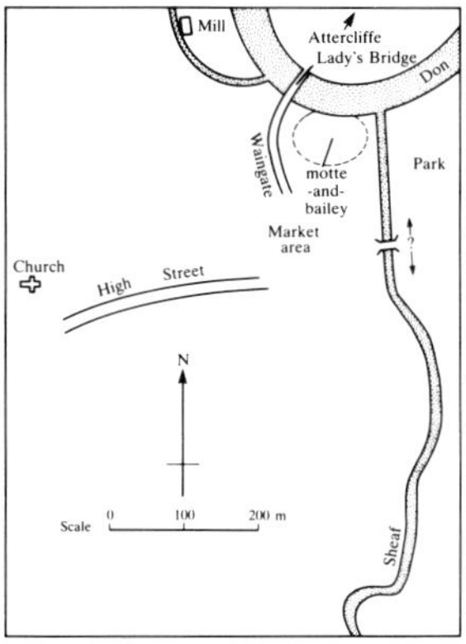

Sheffield, 1116

Compared with the treatment meted out by William on the rest of Yorkshire in his viciously punitive 'harrying of the North', ('It was horrible to observe in houses, streets and roads human corpses rotting' – Symeon of Durham) perhaps only Waltheof got it in the neck. This again shows how the Sheffield area was a relatively secluded borderland: far enough north to be involved in rebellion; just far enough south to avoid the consequences.

As corpses rotted, William's fellow Normans and chosen henchmen became the nobility. Thus by 1116 William de Lovelot became lord of Hallamshire, and he established a castle on the site of the Anglo-Saxon hall. Of motte-and-bailey construction, it was created from upcast earth from a dog-leg of a ditch dug between the Sheaf and Don, with the motte topped by largely wooden defences. Few remains were recorded during the 1927–9 excavations, but a similar site still exists at Bradfield, which would have been a moorland base and refuge for the Norman aristocracy in Sheffield, and is still well worth a visit today.

De Lovelot also drew up Sheffield's first and arguably most logical town plan. He provided for a stone church, later St Peter's and St Paul's, now the city cathedral; a hospice, St Leonard's, beyond the Wicker up Spital Hill (the 'hos' lost from Sheffield tongues through time); a mill at Millsands, surviving as the 'town mill' until the nineteenth century, now Whitbread's Exchange Brewery; and a reliable way across the Don, later named Lady's Bridge.

This bridge was probably as critical to Sheffield's transport infrastructure then as Supertram is now. The only crossing known from the Middle Ages, it opened up the area north of the Don from Stocksbridge to Meadowhall to trade at Sheffield's markets. Doncaster was South Yorkshire's most prosperous medieval town primarily because of its trading position, but Sheffield's position now meant it could become a town, a pre-eminence which had nothing to do with industry. Consequently Ecclesfield remained a village, and despite its better communications, massive investment in the castle at Conisborough, its beautiful bridge, perpendicular church and ecclesiastical prosperity, Rotherham was never to dominate Sheffield's economy.

The present-day street pattern began to emerge, with Waingate skirting the castle's motte-and-bailey (now Castle Market) at a tangent to the High Street, in order to link with Lady's Bridge. Wherever you were in Sheffield you would have been able to see livestock grazing and cornfields; it retained a village character, topographically similar to Grindleford where the B6521 crosses the Derwent in the Peaks.

Lady's Bridge looking upstream. Note three rebuilds to widen this essential crossing. The photograph was probably taken in 1909, judging by the scaffolding in the foreground to construct today's iron-stanchioned pavements. The culvert carries the original town mill's race; behind, iron columns supporting the Exchange Brewery

Houses started to grow beside each other as their tenants started to make a living from the market-place as well as more directly off the land.

Beyond this village two other developments shaped Sheffield's future growth. By 1116 the settlement 'flat spot' east of the town was well-established as a park. Nothing like today's council-run sunbathe and feed the ducks variety, Sheffield Park was the sole domain or *demesne* of the lord of the manor. At 2,461 acres it stretched from what is now the A6178 Attercliffe Road across to Gleadless, and up to the Sheaf on Sheffield's eastern doorstep, as the names Park Hill and Parkway still imply. Largest of all South Yorkshire's medieval parks, and larger than the Lower Don Valley, its origins, its entire shape and features have been swept from the eye within the last century.

A trip to the Duke of Devonshire's estates at Chatsworth will give you a good idea of what Sheffield Park was like. Not simply the deer-herds grazing between well-managed woodlands; these parks were to be increasingly run as businesses as much as for pleasure. True for Chatsworth today, with its farm shop and garden centre; true for Sheffield Park then as its lords, notably the Earls of Shrewsbury followed by the Dukes of Norfolk, were among the first to exploit the coal and iron resources below their deer-herds' feet.

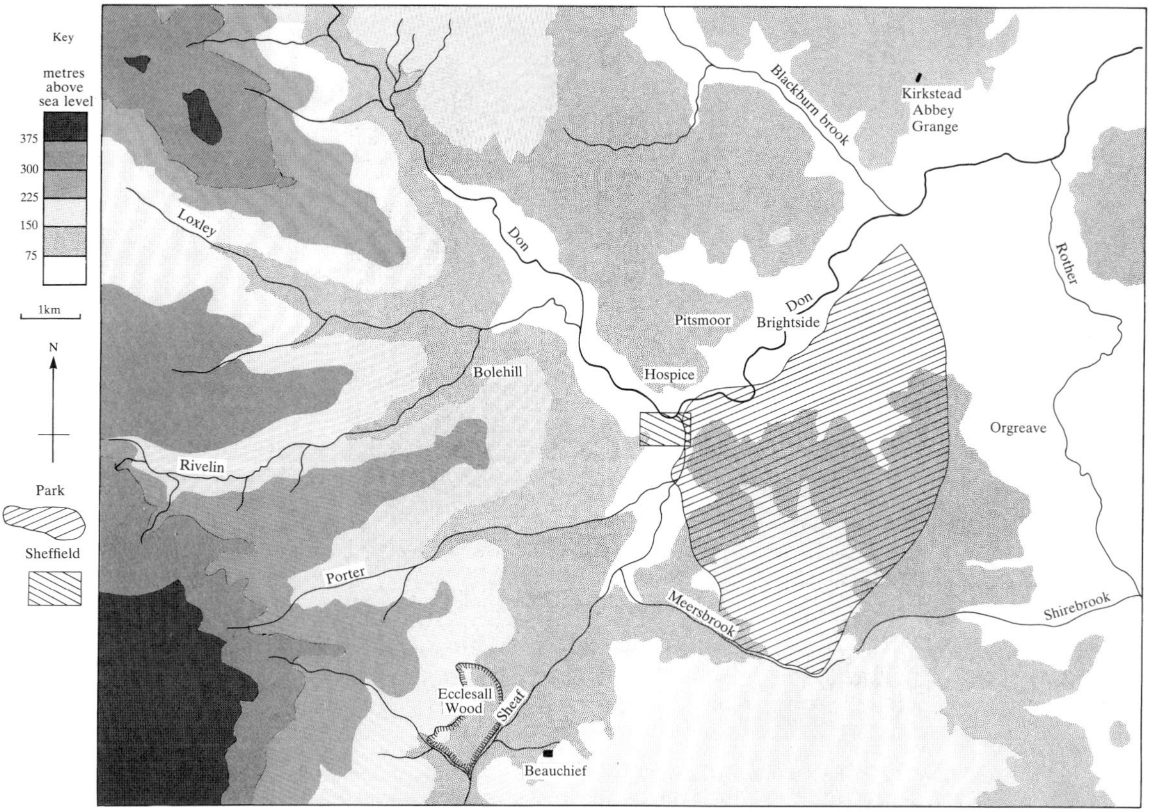

Medieval Sheffield Park

At the same time Sheffield Park was a feudal green belt which denied any eastward expansion of the town until Victoria's jubilee. This economic power and political influence did not die until this century, as the quantity of leasehold properties in Sheffield testifies.

Sheffielders will more readily identify with the other development. A Domesday Book listing of Orgreave already recognized the quarrying of ironstone. On May Day 1161, Richard de Buseli, neighbour and confrère to the de Lovelots, agreed to grant the Cistercian monks from Kirkstead Abbey in Lincolnshire 'a site within the territory of Kimberworth for their houses and an orchard and four forges, to wit, two for smelting iron and two for forging it, whensoever they wished, and leave to dig for ore throughout the territory of that township, so much as would be sufficient for two furnaces.'

The church, monastic orders in particular, was a large landholder and an industrious tenant: de Busli's grant is in keeping with the times. It shows that iron-working was already well known in the area, well enough for outline planning permission to list particulars without further explanation. There was a clear demand or market, since the grant gave the monks a free hand to work to capacity (although what local ironworkers thought of the generous mineral extraction rights can be imagined).

Kirkstead Grange, Kimberworth. Note the small original Norman windows and doorways. Through these twelfth-century monks walked to work to smelt iron

Being built of stone the monks' houses, much modified, survive. Their scale and solidity physically emphasizes that the monks' venture was based upon a sound business plan within a traditional sector rather than an experimental whim and a prayer. It also presages industrialists such as the Walkers, and Rotherham's development as an iron rather than a steel or cutlering centre.

All this activity was the Normans exploiting a fundamentally pre-conquest socio-economic structure: evidence that the conditions of change were defined, or already in place, only to be followed by a hiatus before development – a pattern common to Sheffield's history. There are no Norman new towns here; their only installed settlement lay immediately south of Hallamshire, namely Beauchief Abbey in 1183, a wonderful Normanization of the Anglo-Saxon river name.

Amid the ridge and furrow, commons and woods, iron-workers would ply their trade. 'A third part of all the moneys from all the smithies which shall have farmed out in the park of Shefaud or in any woods of Thomas in Halumsphire . . . and from all smithies hereafter in the said woods and land to be farmed out.' This is from a court settlement of 1268 between the Furnivals, who succeeded the de Lovelots (and whose name is perpetuated in Furnival Street, part of Sheffield's Regency expansion). We can see how ironworking or smithying both thrived and was expected to continue to thrive. From the verb 'farmed out', we can conclude that the work was essentially rural in character, and it is doubtful whether there was then anything like the distinction that we choose to make between 'farming' and 'industry'. Likewise the workers themselves were part-time and seasonal, smithying being part of an annual round of tasks from harvest to harvest, their work places either out-of-doors or in temporary take-overs of rooms.

This may sound casual, but it required team work: charcoal burners, iron-ore diggers, smelters and forgers just to turn rock into iron. That iron would then have to be moulded, bent, beaten and edged to become a tool, to be sold or bartered at market. During this period we start to see surnames which reflect these skills and specialities, such as Naylor. Hallamshire's annual production would scarcely have filled a Bessemer Converter (p. 65), but in terms of a low-capital outlay/high-return industry it was vitally efficient, providing bread on the table and rents for lords even if crops were to fail.

In terms of the landscape there would have been scruffy little hollows or pock-marks, created in a scrabble to dig out the ore, even ignoring upcast coal as waste. The furnaces were built on windward, westerly slopes for the blast (as in the gales whistling up the Rivelin Valley against Bolehill), close to the ore supply (as in Pitsmoor; 'ore-pits' by 1315), if not by charcoal coppices. These were more assiduously managed both as a renewable resource and to produce high-grade fuel. Evidence of ancient coppicing and charcoal burning still survives in Ecclesall Wood, while a good idea of ore extraction can be drawn from similar mini lead quarries in the White Peak, now grassed over, such as on the uplands south of Bakewell. This was an open field, never mind cottage industry.

The razing of de Lovelot's motte-and-bailey in 1266 during Simon de Montfort's campaign to establish a parliament gave notice of Sheffield's economic potential. Instead of remaining a ruin – the eventual fate of Bradfield's motte – the Furnivals immediately applied for a permit to rebuild, which received the royal seal in 1270. This was no earth and wood mound. Its moat cut through rock to a depth of almost 30 ft, the height of an average semi. This was permanently filled with water by clipping the triangle between the Don and the Sheaf. Its walls of well-dressed sandstone still stand 18 ft high, and were at least as thick. Vignettes of the whole were revealed in the 1927–9 excavations by Armstrong. He located a gatehouse and drawbridge footings flanked by one of a pair of intimidating circular bastions, and enough sundry evidence to plot the original layout.

De Lovelot's castle of 1116 protected a village; Furnival's of 1270 dominated a town. Today nothing shows, while beneath Castle Market at least the moat still seems to work according to plan since access to the ruins is prohibited by flooding. In order to appreciate its former might and splendour, look at Newark, where the castle still commands the Trent.

Beneath the market stalls, a section of Sheffield Castle's massive walls

There is the possibility that the town defences extended beyond the castle's massive gate-house. Unpublished work by Clive Hart at the City Museum proposes a walled area running alongside the Sheaf, while hugging the higher ground by Haymarket. This fits John Harrison's account of 1637: '. . . thereof haveing on ye South an outward Court Yard or fould builded round with diverse houses of office as an armory a Granary, Barnes Stables and divers Lodgeings all containeing by measure . . . 4 acres – 00 Roods – 30$^2/_3$ Perches.'

Harrison's measure roughly tallies with the dotted sector abstracted from Gosling's street plan of 1736 (p. 47). A market function is usually ascribed to this area, but this is compatible with Harrison's description, as there would have been something to defend. None of this now survives above ground, even in the way ring-roads mimic Norwich's and York's medieval city walls, but it would entail the walled area of Sheffield stretching from Castle Market almost to Commercial Street.

By about 1300 the maximum extent of English medieval cultivation was reached. To produce more meant intensification and specialization, either on the land or in workshops. It is not difficult to see where Sheffield's future economic development lay. England's population density had roughly doubled since Saxon times. Without accurate censuses, head-counts are hard to calculate, but from two to three figures in Waltheof's time, the poll would be rising through the threes to four. Amongst these were enough 'freemen' (individuals who had paid off

How Sheffield Castle may have looked: a drawing by Martin Davenport

their feudal dues of service to their lords) to warrant the granting of Sheffield's first town charter by the third Thomas Furnival, on 10 August 1297. A practice increasingly common throughout England, this cost the freemen of Sheffield a total of £3 8*s* 9¼*d* per annum, and although the haggling to reach this sum can only be imagined, the key clause appears to be: 'Furthermore, I will and grant for myself and my heirs that the said tenants and their heirs, as well as buyers and sellers, shall everywhere throughout all Hallamshire be quit from all exaction and demand of toll, as they were wont to be in the time of my ancestors, for ever.'

Just as Richard de Buseli's Kimberworth grant to the monks of Kirkstead Abbey recognized and enabled ironworking to develop, this town charter facilitated trade. A year earlier Furnival had gained the right to hold a second weekly market and two annual fairs, so it is clear he understood the advantages of free trade, and to whom. Furnival retained full administrative and judicial control through his manorial court: Sheffield was a town run by a manor.

Economically this worked. Sheffield seems to have missed the early fourteenth century's lengthy slump, if not the Black Death. By the time of the poll tax returns of 1379 (levied to fund a rematch with

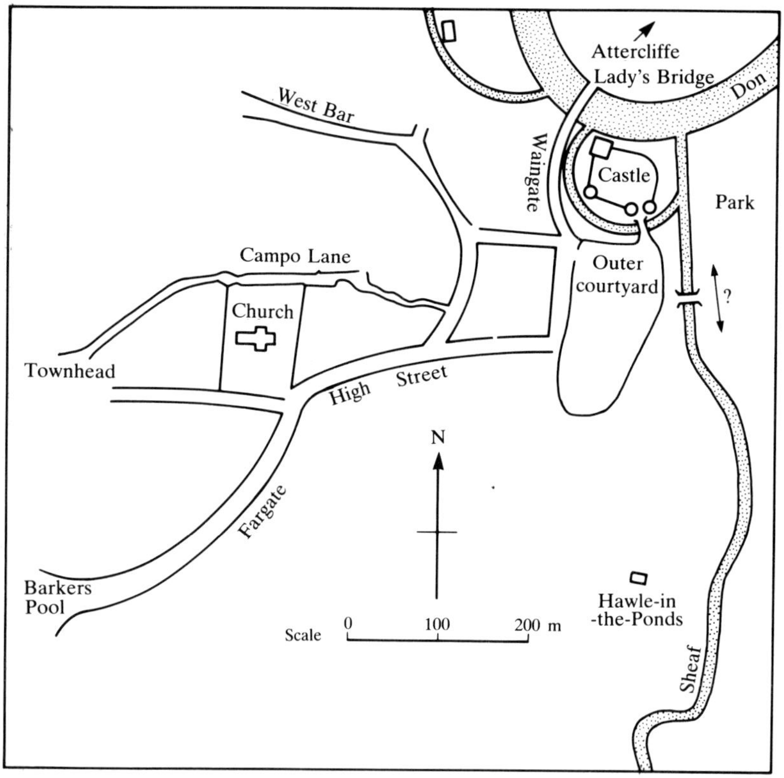

Sheffield, 1497, including castle 'outward courtyard'

France at war, and triggering the Peasants' Revolt of 1381: cause and effect of the 1989–93 poll tax is small beer), Sheffield had become the West Riding's third richest, or most honest, town.

Sheffield's name spread. In 1340 a Tower of London inventory includes a 'cultellum de Sheffeld', together with, for example, 'XX cutellos' from Ashbourne. However, it appears to be quality, not quantity which is associated with Sheffield's name. Exactly what sort of quality is harder to say. By 1387 it needed no explanation from Chaucer in his *Reeve's Tale*: 'A Sheffeld thwitel baar he in his hose.' 'Thwitel' means knife, and the 'he' in question is a round-faced, flat-nosed miller known as a scornful Simkin, a swaggering nuisance at markets and a cheat. In other words, Chaucer knew this sort of person would choose to display Made in Sheffield against his thigh.

Chaucer also knew his audience would recognize the reference, which implies a regular distribution of knives, a consequence of the freeing-up of skills and trade embodied in Furnival's town charter a century earlier. Although these references are to Sheffield, the crafts-

10 August 1297. Thomas Furnival seals Sheffield's first town charter

men are recorded evenly throughout the town and Hallamshire. There are no references to men who are cutlers in Sheffield, and only four in the rest of Hallamshire. Sheffield itself was a market-place rather than a hotbed of manufacture.

From these data we can draw a picture of a fundamentally part-time industry dotted across the parishes, with each worker specializing in his own part of the whole, which came to market under the castle walls. Distribution would be local, then regional, then national, and finally international as Sheffield's inherent transport deficit was overcome by the quality of the embedded labour values. Chaucer catches the time twixt regional and national marketing.

What sort of knife would have rubbed against the miller's thigh? The question of whether it was steel or not is probably anachronistic. Steel for us is a type of metal, then it was more a quality. The iron was repeatedly heated and beaten over glowing charcoal, to remove impurities and add carbon until the quality of metal required for the next stage was judged right. It relied upon experience as much as skill, and such knowledge was handed down from father to son, master to apprentice. With each generation the skills and products became finer, yet it was never to go far beyond an unwritten art before Benjamin Huntsman's time in the late eighteenth century. It did not need to. Indeed the hands-on empirical approach of highly specialized and skilled crafts runs right through Sheffield tool and cutlery manufacture however large – or small – the workshops became.

By 1497 when the bridge across the Don was rebuilt and named Lady's Bridge because of a chapel on its far side, Sheffield was the size and shape it was to retain until the mid-eighteenth century. For a more life-size picture of Sheffield then, travel on from Grindleford to Bakewell. Here you have the river, bridge, the park (Chatsworth) to the east, the steep hills and tall-spired church, and twiddly-diddly lanes and alleys. Visit on Mondays for market and the crush of livestock will literally add to the aroma. A deeper feel of medieval urban farming can be gained from the Heeley City Farm (p. 117). Unlike 1066, from the town centre in 1497 you could hardly see a field, but your nose would smell farmyards, not ironworks.

On the south edge of town, well beyond any defensive wall, stood the Hawle in the Ponds, a fine L-shaped squire's house, now truncated and transformed into the Queen's Head pub. Today it looks out of place, even though still alone. This is an artefact, the sole secular artefact standing *in situ* of Sheffield's medieval legacy. Although street patterns can be glimpsed here and there nothing else stands proud because of urban development, planned and unplanned, which never looked back at the past until the last ten years.

Unlike the axe which ended Waltheof's life, the blades which hewed the timbers of the Hawle in the Ponds were probably made in Sheffield.

Mary Turton, former buffer-girl, demonstrating her craft before taking part in the opening of the World Student Games

Hawle in the Ponds, waiting at a past-stop

Sheffield
Interchange

CHAPTER FIVE

From Manor to Manufacture

Between the cock's crow and the milk-herd lowing back to pasture, Mary, Queen of Scots may have heard strange faint sounds begin in the valley below from her prison quarters at Sheffield Manor in 1569. To their makers they were already deafeningly familiar. A century earlier, around the time the Hawle in the Ponds was built, Sheffield's metal industry underwent its first radical change for at least 500 years.

Since George Eliot wrote *The Mill on the Floss*, water wheels have been associated with bucolic nostalgia rather than engines of industrialization. But as Mary Walton (p. 117) pointed out in 1948, the coming of water power to the smith's rather than miller's elbow is dramatic and important. The wheeze of furnace bellows, the twanging thud of trip hammers, the singing buzz of a grinder's wheel, each driven by rippling streams rather than rippling muscle.

The plethora of water wheels meant cheap, clean and ecologically

The ruins of Sheffield Manor, from a print published by D. Martin, 1791

sound power. It required investment in plant: not simply the dam and lake, wheel and wheel-house, but also the grinding wheels, axles, bearings, pulleys, belts, cams, bellows and valves. This was basically stone, wood and leather technology, but enshrining a fundamental engineering principle of industrialization – the conversion of one form of power into another. A water-driven blast furnace would have been as magical a sight in 1600 as a horseless carriage three centuries later.

The Pennine watershed was also exploited both north and south, to industrialize the wool trade, with similar commercial and social implications. But water power was slower to take off than in Bradford, Halifax and Huddersfield. At first sight this seems to be a simple function of population, and its rapid growth in the seventeenth century.

The spread of wheels gave the valleys a new identity and focus, perhaps in the same way as the weavers' villages on the Colne and Aire to the north or, across a larger area, the mining communities in the Victorian Rhondda of South Wales. The wheels went almost into the centre of Sheffield; the Hawle in the Ponds wasn't to stay on its own for long, indeed a tannery developed nearby, ideally located to exploit the livestock market, copious water supply, and the wearing out of leather drivebelts. The number of mills led to water shortages, so that full millponds were stealthily diverted or vigilantly patrolled. The one area to remain relatively unchanged in this period was the Lower Don Valley.

More power: the grinder could concentrate on sharpening more blades better. More precise and controllable power: no praying the wind wouldn't change speed or direction in the middle of a furnace blast on Bole Hill. At each stage the product could reach guaranteed standards, and quality control became far less haphazard.

It also meant that the various processes could be brought to a single site. We may not be sure when iron-smelting started at Bolehills, but it had died out by the 1500s, leaving behind the wind and Sheffield's first post-industrial landscape. Although the individual craftsmen still worked for themselves, they now worked closer together at each mill. This led to a greater sharing of ideas and experiences, and grievances too. This geographical concentration of the means of production is the embryo of huge factories and labour forces.

Shepherd Wheel (p. 117) represents the first stage in this process, a small wheel solely for grinding and buffing edged tools; individual 'hulls' rented out by the day, week or season to individual craftsmen. Wortley Top Forge (p. 117) formed part of the Spencer Syndicate, a seventeenth-century coalition of local ironmasters who were investing capital as well as labour, and attempting to control prices as well as the quality of the iron sold on to the nailers, cutlers and scythemakers.

Abbeydale Hamlet: workers' houses

Abbeydale Hamlet (p. 117) illustrates the next step. Capital was invested in workers as well as plant, to pay their wages and house their families, all on the one site, focused upon a single product – scythes. Beginning in the 1780s it is among the last of the water-powered sites, yet the first of Sheffield's factories.

Although the place of work altered, the manner of work (individual crafts producing individual objects) remained the same. What economic and social forces forged this intensification and commercialization of a medieval cottage industry?

A ruin since 1706, Sheffield Manor (p. 117) signified the change from the medieval to a renaissance world. Its foundation stone laid around 1525, gone are all ideas of defence and refuge imbued in the town's castle, replaced by vistas of elegance within gardened surrounds. To appreciate the heyday of Sheffield Manor, watch Peter Greenaway's film *The Draughtsman's Contract* or visit Haddon Hall on the A6 between Matlock and Bakewell, a similar establishment that probably incorporated the work of identical journeymen masons. Each of these was employed, via a factor, by the Talbot family, the Earls of Shrewsbury, whose estates and influence ranged across England. Following the Wars of the Roses, power struggles between the aristocracy were settled by economic bargaining rather than arranged marriages and pitched battles.

Shepherd Wheel. The rod running through the roof to the wheel controls water flow – like a car accelerator pedal

Although Sheffield remained manorial, the means of control were no longer military might and allegiance by feud, but rentals, leases and direct exploitation of the land. Coal-mining, which had been begun as early as the thirteenth century by the monks at Beauchief Abbey, started to take off in the sixteenth century, because of the lack of wood to keep both domestic and metalworking grates glowing, and regular cartloads of coal trundled from Sheffield Park pits across the new Sheaf bridge of 1597 to town householders' doorsteps. Francis Bacon described the Earl of Shrewsbury as 'a great collier'.

Coal, yes, but the Earls of Shrewsbury, like the Dukes of Norfolk after them, did not try their hands at manufacturing. In common with the land-owning aristocracy they maintained their wealth through estate management, and a coal-pit in one field would be viewed in much the same way as wheat in another. The Earl's rents and the plant invested in the water wheels, used to manufacture items at economic prices, ensured that craftsmen were forced to go one of two ways – either to invest in plant and rents, or work for those who had invested. This is the start of the classic separation in a capitalist society of the worker from the means of production. Instead of exchanging the products of their labour at the market-place, their labour itself was a product.

The collier soon had to work for the pit-operator (because the investment is in the extraction, not the product). Not so the metalworker, whose hands, not geology, determine the product. Although South Yorkshire is associated with mining as much as steel, these fundamental differences are reflected in the very different labour and social histories of steel- and coal-working communities. The pit-villages east of the Sheaf and Don were, and still are, very different from the metal-working valleys to their west. Once more Sheffield lies on a border, this time drawn through labour relations.

Independent metal-workers survived, indeed flourished, by producing very high-quality items – as they still do today. This is embodied in the formation of the Cutlers' Company. With its grand Victorian hall opposite the cathedral, it became a powerful business assembly. Its origins were rather different.

> To that court came William Elles and took of the lord a private mark by himself for marking iron knives, such a mark as ▶◀, to have and to use by himself: and if any other person should strike that mark and thereupon be convicted by verdict he should lose to the lords XX shillings, and make amendement to the injured party; and he gave to the lord 1*d* of yearly rent.
>
> 2 October 1554

This fragment of a manorial roll shows that the certification of cutlers and their wares was already being laid down within the earl's

Cutlers' Halls. The first, 1638. The third and present, *c.* 1900

court, and the said William Elles paid 1*d* a year for the service. By 1565, 'constitutiones, ordainces and devises' became law, to regulate what may now be properly called an industry. They ratified a seven-year apprenticeship, and forbade either finishing or providing half-finished work to outsiders. These measures reflect a strong degree of isolation and protectionism: in the next century Sheffield cutlers found it difficult to break into a London market dominated by their rivals, and even today the Sheffield business community sometimes feels isolated from its peers.

Those cutlers with marks, and not all would have had them, would have been increasingly dedicated: full-time professionals with apprentices and order books, a far cry from Chaucer's day, where the 'thwitel' rather than its maker was recognized. By 1578 there were sixty marks listed on the manorial rolls, and 1590 saw a separate court for cutlery business. It seems to have worked, for also in 1590 Peter Bales, an Elizabethan equivalent to a journalist, wrote: 'first therefore be the choice of your penknife, a right Sheffield knife is best.' The cutlers' court was all about that right.

Although the court's effect was similar to a medieval craft guild, it was as much a part of the lord's domain as his castle or manor. To a freeman and guild member this would have been almost as unrecognizable as the function of today's Cutlers' Company as a trade union is to a shop steward. This is another instance of a hiatus in Sheffield development. The material conditions for a guild of knifesmiths were defined by the time the first grinding wheel was turning in the fifteenth century, if not before. Not until the 1620s did the cutlers approach parliament. The Earls of Shrewsbury, if not the Dukes of Norfolk, seem to have taken an interest almost as keen as the blades the cutlers made. Their numbers and the complexity of their disputes as much as an intrinsic desire for independence led to the Act of Parliament in 1624 to form The Company of Cutlers in Hallamshire.

Ironically the establishment of this Company was a nail in the coffin of feudal Hallamshire as a politically powerful administrative unit, mrroring the establishment of the Twelve Capital Burgesses and Commonalty of the Town and Parish of Sheffield, decreed by Queen Mary in 1554. A consequence of the Reformation, this was a less democratic yet more ecclesiastical replacement of Furnival's charter of 1297; but the burgesses were still only responsible for provision of services such as upkeep of the roads and the poor. The town remained governed by its lord and, viewed in that light, the Cutlers' Company is the first autonomous organization in Sheffield.

Not that the Company kept to its own rules. Throughout the seventeenth century legislation geared to protect an isolated trade was broken by cutlers keen to expand. Although they knew exactly what they wanted to make and how to make it, there was no clear or agreed policy of what to do once the blades were made. This lack of a unified commercial talent contrasts strongly with the woollen industry of the West Riding, and evidence of the mercantile rise of Leeds, Wakefield, Halifax and later Bradford is to be found in the 1686 War Office returns of guest-beds and stables, which placed Sheffield fifth in the Riding.

Quite often this is put down to the transport difficulties of Sheffield's geography. However, these predicated the size and quality of the town's products, small and good, not the town itself. Certainly the roads were good enough for the delivery of slates to roof the first Cutlers' Hall in 1638, and trade was healthy enough to pay for it. When Gosling drew the earliest surviving town map in 1736, however, it still retained its medieval shape and much of its character.

This retention was not just physical, with a Church Lane where 'Roofs nearly meeting, a dark dreary retreat, might justly be styled the robber's retreat', and a reliance upon wells and cess-pits for water and sanitation, but also economic, where cutlers made nails in hard times, competing with the humble nailers they never admitted into their Company.

There were exceptions. The Spencer syndicate made and traded iron throughout the area and sold nails in the capital. The Blythes of Norton Lees were more individual. The elder William Blythe, as well as rebuilding the 'Bishop's House' at Meersbrook Park (p.117), was

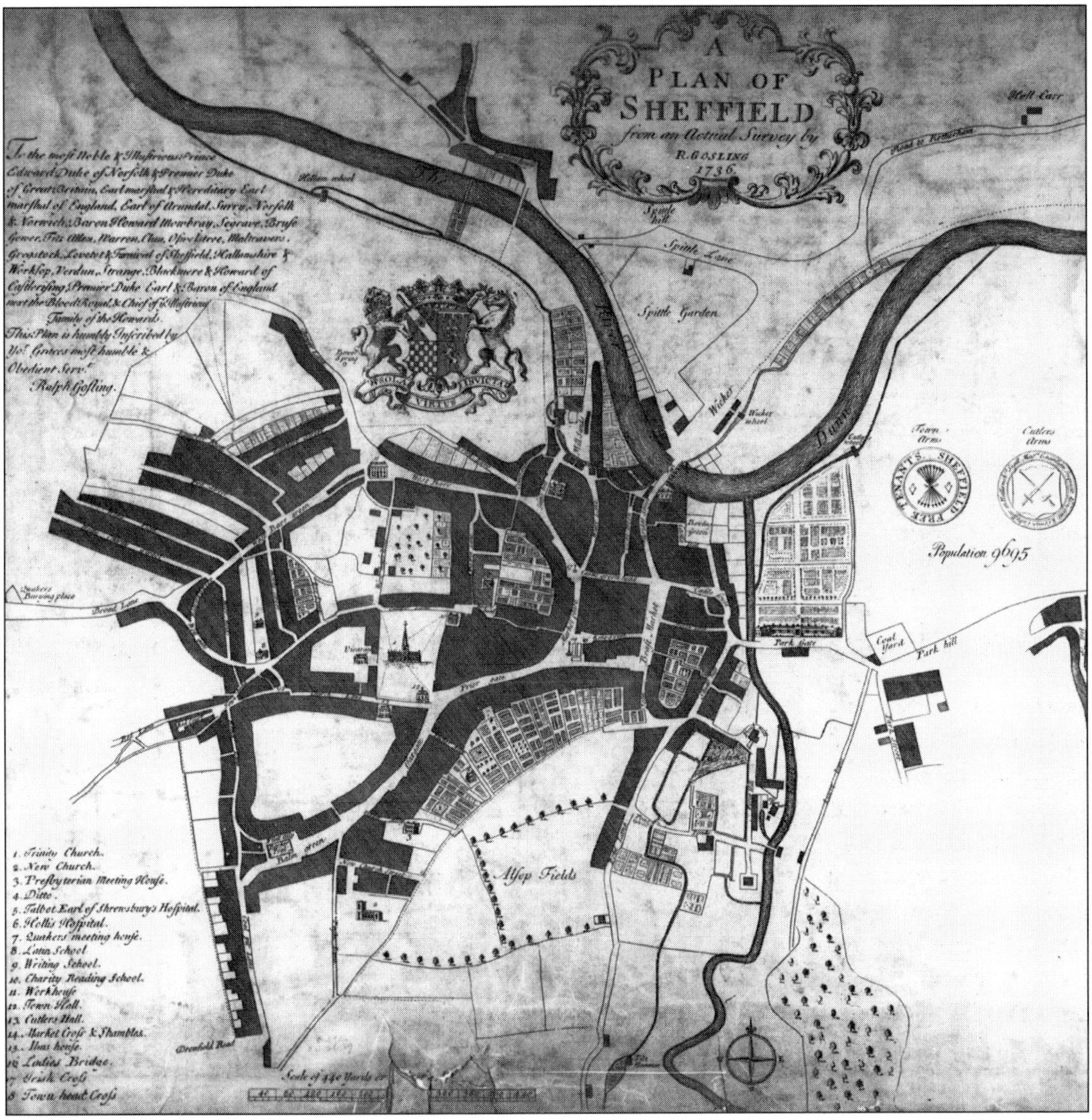

Sheffield, 1736

a farmer and merchant. His estate when he died in 1631/2 was one-third farm, two-thirds scythes. He was renting space at the Heeley mill and smithies nearby for craftsmen to make the scythes on a sub-contract or outwork basis. Blythe had a thousand scythes in stock, 2½ tons of iron, with a quarter of its value in steel.

William, his son, carried on the business. At his death in 1665/6 he both stock warehoused in Wakefield, Boroughbridge, York and Beverley and money owing from York, Morpeth and Newcastle.

Bishop's House, 1823, drawing by Edward Blore

Although the production line is still pre-industrial, the Blythes had developed a tiny business empire. It is no accident this was in scythes. First, there was a steady and continuous demand to cut the wheat and hay. Second, a scythe blade was not too heavy to transport long distances. Third, it was made from sandwiching steel between iron, which required skill and was ideally suited to water power for hammering and grinding. The Sheaf valley became famous for its scythes, and they are still made at its Abbeydale Hamlet (p. 117).

The mix of iron and steel is particularly important. Sheffield was not yet a steel producer. Instead, during the sixteenth century steel was imported at first from Spain and Austria, each on the borders of the Arabic world, where steel manufacture developed early in the medieval period. A wonderful apocryphal tale relates how Richard the Lionheart bragged to Saladin by breaking an anvil in half with his mighty two-handed iron broadsword. Mightily impressed, with a flick of the wrist Saladin lifted a veil from a dancing girl and cut it in two while it fluttered in mid-air. Sheffield was far from these metallurgical developments, and Sheffield ores, with their phosphor, were hard to make into steel. To slake the cutlers' thirst for quality, from the seventeenth century continental iron from Sweden was increasingly imported, right through to this century. But by 1709 at least Samuel Shore had realized how to make steel on a commercial basis in Sheffield itself.

This is arguably the start of Steel City, but certainly the continuation of a dialectic between metal manufacturer and metal user. Even today the individual cutlers are ever critical of their raw materials, yet their constant demand for metals with exact qualities brought steel, then steel-making to Sheffield, to provide a craftsman's spur to technological improvement.

The town was becoming increasingly monothetic in its economic base. Not so with religion: the sons of the second William Blythe, who had been a captain in Cromwell's army, were dissenters, who began Sheffield's radical tradition. The town's nature was changing. The castle, physical and metaphysical bastion of manorial control, fell in the Civil War, to be obliterated directly afterwards, its stonework used to rebuild the townspeople's individual old timber-framed houses. Ironically, none of these rebuilds survive either.

Nor do the dissenters' earliest meeting places. But they thrived in Sheffield, perhaps in reaction to the town's continued manorial control following the Restoration and the orthodox Church's declining secular powers. The movement covered all people, and it became a focus for radical development. Today this is best seen in the number, size and spiritual splendour of Sheffield's Methodist churches.

Although the levels of poverty and health were not much worse, or better, than elsewhere, neither the burgesses nor the manor could provide a regular and accountable system of relief, to the poor or better off. For example, a doctor had to be summoned from Doncaster to treat one of the Duke of Norfolk's entourage in 1639. In 1681 the Twelve Capital Burgesses' power was effectively taken over by thirteen Town Trustees, who were at least notionally more democratic and effective, building the first Town Hall (long-since gone and forgotten)

Walkley Methodist chapel turns to pumping iron in Steel City

in 1700 within the south-east corner of the churchyard at the junction of High Street and Fargate. The centre of town was inching its way up the hill from the original Saxon crossing of the Sheaf.

Its control lay in an amalgam of the Duke of Norfolk, the Church of England, the Cutlers' Company and radical dissenters, with individual protagonists and antagonists from one to four of these camps. Add to this loyalties to the smaller communities, such as Attercliffe, Ecclesall and Heeley, outside the town but within its influence, and it is easy enough to imagine the confused crossfire of local politics, so very different to today's polarized debates from entrenched positions. It is recorded in the reaction to the 1665 Hearth Tax, which hit Sheffield badly since the smiths' hearths were to be assessed individually. No one wanted to pay 2*s* per hearth per year forever, yet everyone had their own way of protesting, with the upshot that Sir John Reresby, a Thryburgh JP, and Francis Jessop of Broom Hall were petitioned to plea together on the cutlers' behalf, although they had previously come to blows! The Hearth Tax stayed until 1688.

From its returns of 1672 the town's population was probably still less than three thousand. By 1736 it had trebled to 10,121, with 90 per cent of migrant apprentices coming from less than a day's ride away. Although the town still retained its medieval layout, it had become a manufacturing centre increasingly distinct from its agricultural hinterland. The smith who worked for William Blythe in 1631 may also have worked in the fields surrounding Sheffield. The smiths of 1736 may only have been able to look.

In the longer term, religious dissent and factional politics were ways of coming to terms with this enormous switch. They provided an impetus to establish schools, almshouses, even a book trade; a network of social and cultural resources whose origins today only survive on paper. The town no longer needed ducal patronage, and it is almost by the way that the manor fell into ruin by 1706.

These sudden and dramatic social changes rested upon an industry unaltered in principle from Mary, Queen of Scots' day. Refined and intensified, the smith of 1631 would have easily adjusted to the work place of 1736. When John Wesley preached in Sheffield in 1743 he faced 'the largest congregation I ever saw on a weekday'. This demonstrated the strength of Methodism, and its universality. Everyone was prepared, and allowed, to stop work and listen.

Wesley also looked over open fields. The rest of Paradise Square would not be built until 1771. By then the economic infrastructure to transform a manufacturing town into an industrial city was also in place. Sheffield 1893 would be unrecognizable.

CHAPTER SIX

Steel by the Yard

In itself Sheffield Plate is now a minor historical curiosity, a way of making pretend-silver which endured little more than a hundred years. Yet it encapsulates the longer history of mass-produced Sheffield steel, while the economic exploitation of Thomas Boulsover's accidental discovery in 1743 both presaged and helped put into place the conditions for the massive steel works a century later.

By a mixture of accident and design, Boulsover developed a method of hot-plating copper with silver, so that finished articles could be made from sheet plate, rather than laboriously adding the silver to the finished base article. This meant that more attractive pieces could be manufactured more quickly. It came at the right time; the market for dining-room rather than kitchen ware was expanding, and Sheffield Plate with Sheffield cutlery was selected to match the fine china mass-produced at the Staffordshire Potteries. (See the chronological displays which illustrate this point exactly at the City Museum, p. 117). Sheffield had become literally a household name.

Although incorporated into the Cutlers' Company this form of business was different, in that it required initial capital investment. In the sixteenth century William Blythe's stocks of scythes were built up gradually, a lifetime's endeavour bringing together work from countless different workers and sites. Boulsover's market rather than technique demanded more rapid expansion. Boulsover restricted himself to buttons, others such as Joseph Hancock diversified the product range. Hancock also built the Old Park Silver Rolling Mills on the Don specifically to roll plate by water power for other craftsmen and works. By 1773 Sheffield needed its own assay office to hallmark silverware.

Sheffield Plate tea kettle and stand, made by Wilkinson in 1830

The factory system was beginning. A new sort of occupation was being created. The Blythes were farmers and factors, the Boulsovers and Hancocks were industrialists as much as craftsmen. Where did their capital come from? How did they learn when, where and what to invest? Economics, the most inexact of sciences, was still in swaddling clothes as Adam Smith tried to work out for himself how capitalism worked – or didn't. Throughout the country these were experimental days.

Due primarily to its isolation, Sheffield's mercantile base developed well after Yorkshire's, and Britain's other major towns. There was nothing like the tradition of international trade as at Bristol, or indeed Gloucester. Ironically, while the medieval town lies below ground and not one back-to-back still stands, the centre of this backwater development survives virtually intact.

In 1736 Joseph Broadbent built a row of houses just down from Campo Lane. Although to a pattern, they were each built separately to order. If the land lease was speculative, the houses weren't. Today we tend to see this as a unitary development called Paradise Square. Look more closely and the square isn't even rectangular, but shaped to fit pre-existing old field boundaries. Into this 'square' we read a thriving business community. In 1736 Broadbent merely extended his interests to housing.

By the 1740s Broadbent, the Kenyons and Roebucks were travelling abroad, to establish agents in Germany, Russia and Spain. They were dealing directly with their markets, rather than through middlemen in other English cities. It worked. Joseph Broadbent died in 1761 worth £20,000.

If this hadn't been so successful, Broadbent's son Thomas would hardly have been able in 1771 to add three more sides to his father's row of houses, thus putting Paradise Square on the map. In order to help and profit from others needing commercial services, Benjamin Roebuck established Sheffield's first bank in 1770, closely followed by Thomas Broadbent's in 1774. They invested in the metal trades. Roebuck's brother John, educated at Sheffield Grammar School and a

Paradise Square in the snow, 1979. In 1743, John Wesley preached from its highest doorstep

physician, became interested enough in metallurgy to help set up the Carron ironworks on the Forth estuary in Scotland, later famed for its Carronade naval cannon and original telephone kiosks. The first instance of a Sheffield business investing outside Hallamshire, it predates the enormous expansion of Sheffield-based industrial conglomerates such as Vickers a century later.

Although each bank immediately ran into serious difficulties, Broadbent's crashing in 1780, they provided a new method of business development. In future, to expand in Sheffield you would need capital to enter the industrial market-place, as well as skills at the work place.

It also provided a model of personal development. Unlike the Blythes, who were initially farmers, these men's origins lay in the Cutlers' Company, their forebears serving apprenticeships; the merchants and early steelmasters named Shore going back as far as 1440. Financial success also replicated the manorial system, the Shores, Broadbents and Roebucks building themselves rural mansions. Sheffield's later Victorian industrialists simply worked on a grander scale in terms of the size of their works and homes.

Ringinglow Toll House. Sited on a Y-junction and designed to watch and charge traffic from Sheffield, either towards Chapel-en-le-Frith or Buxton

If Paradise Square put Sheffield on to the economic map, its geographical isolation was still apparent. Throughout the country highways underwent commercialization through turnpiking. In the Sheffield area this earliest system of national road pricing initially integrated the town into the pre-existing network, the Sheffield–-Chesterfield–Derby road first to be turnpiked in 1756. Not until 1821, two years after the Sheffield Canal reached the town centre, and just nine years before George Stephenson's pioneering Liverpool and Manchester Railway, was there a turnpike road from Sheffield to Glossop (via Snake Pass) and on directly to Manchester. In this region roadbuilders respected Sir Cyril Fox's highland–lowland division until the M62.

Turnpikes ensured a reliable travel network so that goods could be ordered and dispatched according to a schedule rather than hope. Meetings between interested parties were more by appointment rather than chance. On the other hand, they added to the unit transport costs, which militated against the smaller trader. Like cars in our own era, for those who could afford the tolls the country became smaller, their ambit larger; for those who could not, the reverse became true.

Part-time metal workers felt the pinch in another area. Just as Paradise Square enclosed agricultural land, the enclosure acts which followed entailed the loss of common grazing rights for the smallholder. Today the drystone walls dipping down from the Pennine moors are viewed as part of the natural landscape, unchanged since the sixth day of creation, and therefore to be revered and conserved at all costs. In fact they were largely built in a massive Georgian job creation scheme, to provide work for the rural dispossessed after Parliament's first act of privatization. Feeling this pinch in both the metalwork and agricultural spheres, the part-time workers who had established and consolidated Sheffield's industry for at least four centuries, were doomed. The underlying agricultural nature of the Lower Don Valley is emphasized by the fact that Attercliffe was the last parish to be surveyed by the enclosure commissioners between 1810 and 1819.

Turnpikes and enclosures were fundamentally national phenomena. Inland navigations were prompted more by local interests. The development of the Sheffield Canal Company illustrates the fragility of the town's investment economy and the divergent goals of those who controlled it. The threefold increase in population between 1672 and 1736 continued, fed by food coming through enclosures and turnpikes to the markets which spread over Lady's Bridge and down the Wicker. It was clear to all that a bottleneck lay in moving foreign iron and steel in, as well as Made in Sheffield products out. The transport penalty was doubled.

As early as 1698 the Cutlers' Company and town trustees shared the idea of stretching the navigable Don to Tinsley. This co-operation was partly a single body of people wearing two hats, but it testifies a more outward looking approach. Parliament did not agree to share the vision until 1726, and it was then hard to gain sufficient investment. Consequently the canal was paying a dividend by 1732 yet did not reach Tinsley before 1751. The politics behind this were complicated by the Duke of Norfolk's and Earl Fitzwilliam's conflicting coal interests and the fear that each would lose his market share to the other. A canal worried the wharfholders and carriers of Bawtry and Doncaster, not to mention the Sheffield mill-users employing the same finite head of water.

Whatever the strengths, weaknesses, opportunities and threats, the canal camp just did not have the political or financial clout. Elsewhere canals and navigable rivers assisted the growth of mass production in factories, in Sheffield this continued lacuna protected the hand-made, high-quality profile of its industry, yet provided an incentive to provide better quality raw materials cheaper. This can be seen by the relocation of Samuel Walker's iron and steel business from the 1741 Grenoside works to the more famous Masborough site on the navigable Don in 1746. Having direct access to wharfage, Rotherham developed an iron grate industry which Sheffield found hard to emulate.

Benjamin Huntsman was hardly interested in iron grates. A clock-

The dream of 1698 in 1992. Old steel warehousing awaits canal basin redevelopment

EFFINGHAM LANE 4
100
8
THOS TURTON & SONS
LTD
WAREHOUSE
No 1.

maker, he was originally keen to improve the quality of steel springs when he began experiments in 1740. The accepted cementation process was expensive in fuel and time, and produced variable quality blister steel, which needed reheating and hammering to become usable. Huntsman took the blister steel and, using coke instead of charcoal, reheated it within a clay crucible – to 1600°C! He pushed furnace and crucible technology towards space-age temperatures and quality.

Clay crucibles after firing with their iron shaping plugs: at Abbeydale Hamlet. Rightly the symbol for steel manufacture, the clay of Benjamin Huntsman's invention separated heat from the fire. These are test-tubes for industrial metallurgy

Huntsman was a persevering man. Neighbours must have doubted his sagacity, if not sanity, as experiment after failed experiment piled up in his backyard. However, he stands astride the old empirical techniques and the metallurgical methods of the next century. A radical Quaker, he refused membership of the Royal Society, yet he turned steel manufacture from a craft to a science.

Some local cutlers were sceptical of the new steel. Equally there is a story of Samuel Walker indulging in industrial espionage to obtain Huntsman's secret. Perhaps no one realized that the steel and cutlery trades were about to go their own separate ways.

In 1751 Huntsman and two assistants worked to an annual capacity of 8 tons. Sheffield's first trade directory of 1774 listed four steel producers; in 1856 there were 135, including all the great names. Each used Huntsman's secret: as the poundage of crucibles increased, so did the importance of steel manufacture as opposed to its use. Huntsman's crucible provided the technological impetus and shape to Steel City.

The canal, reservoirs, development plots, its very street plan had left behind the town's medieval antecedents. The need for building land was exploited by the Duke of Norfolk. To the south of the core of narrow lanes and alleys, his factor Vincent Eyre planned a new development upon classical rectangular lines, to be carried out between 1776 and 1793 by William Fairbank. This ran from Norfolk Street, by the 1896 Town Hall, to St Mary's Road, a late 1970s fragment of a still incomplete inner ring road. The substance of Eyre's and Fairbank's conception has been effectively obliterated by post-Second World War planning policy. Since the 1960s, Moore Street, Charter Row, Furnival Gate, Arundel Gate, the widening of Eyre Street and the Town Hall extension have wrecked a more graceful and delicate weave, just as surely as replacing a Georgian fireplace and cornice with a coal-effect electric fire and artex ceiling. Today Leader House on Surrey Street is a refugee, as isolated as the Hawle in the Ponds.

This is not to say that Eyre's and Fairbank's actuality matched a Bath, or even a Buxton. John Leather's 1823 map highlights land for building; it is a developers' prospectus as much as a topographical

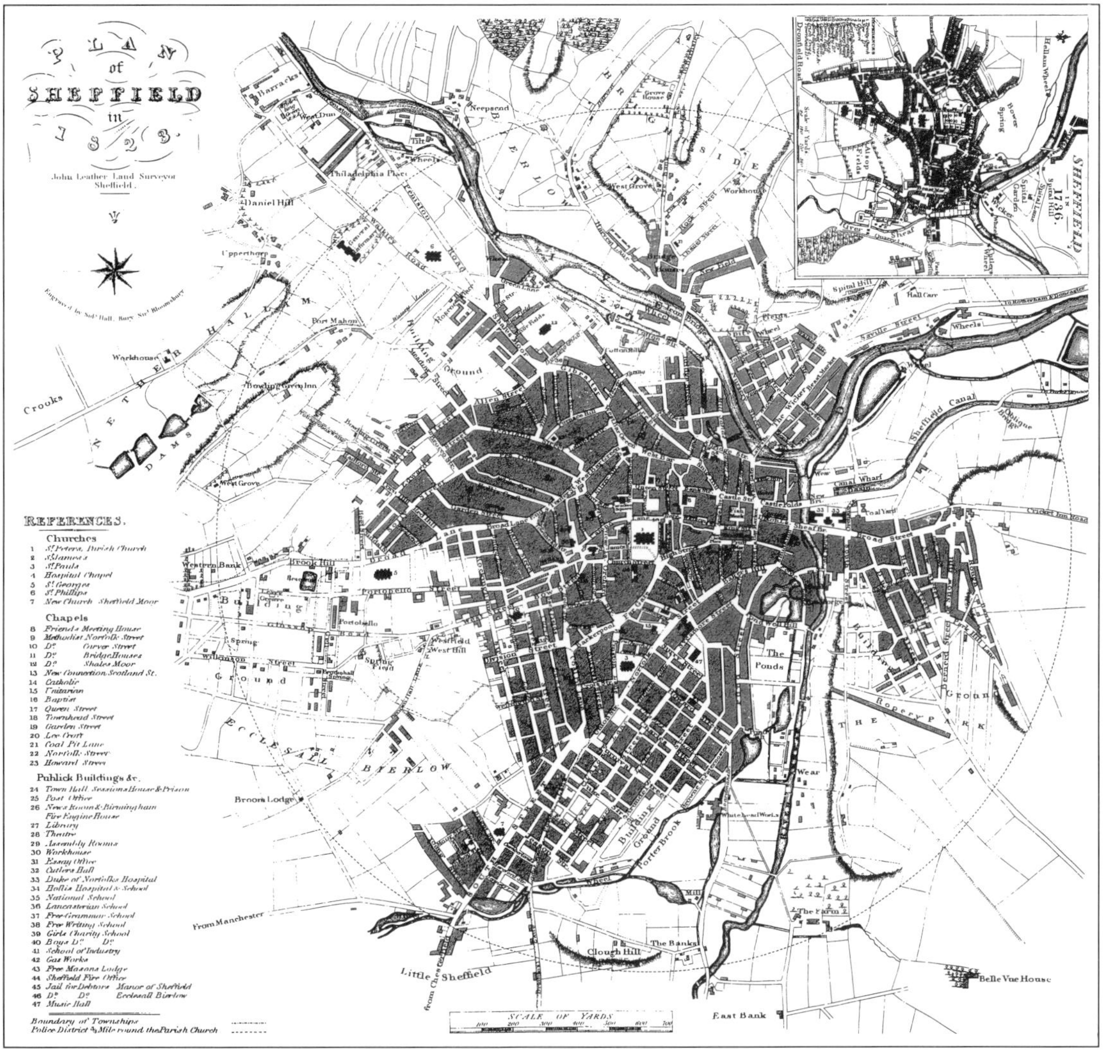

Sheffield, 1823. Leather's map is a development prospectus, as the 1736 inset and 'Building Ground' shows

record. The street patterns were controlled, but the buildings seemed an irregular mix between residential and industrial use – largely because the two were still considered acceptable neighbours if not completely interchangeable properties. Small purpose-built factories share gables with terraced houses, reiterating a typical pattern seen throughout Sheffield.

The first exclusively residential development was Park Hill during the 1790s. Again under the Duke of Norfolk's aegis and within his park, these terraces were for those who worked in town or the Duke's coalpits. Virtually nothing survives, unlike the Broomhall Estate

Sheffield Magnet Company, Broad Lane. Classic central street frontage – house and works sited together

which was just being laid out in 1823. This was to be gated, probably to keep out wandering sheep as much as vagrants.

Eyre and Fairbank, or the Duke of Norfolk's Development Corporation, seem a success. It took thirty-five years to develop Paradise Square. Eyre's design, as large again as the entire old town, was virtually full in seventeen. This shows how much more capital was available in the town by 1823, despite the adverse effect of the Napoleonic Wars, only now it was firmly in the hands, or more precisely the pockets and pocket-books, of industrialists and their bankers, instead of their duke. Two centuries after the international mercantilism of Elizabeth I, Sheffield was economically free of a feudal overlord.

The canal age at last reached the town in 1819, bearing witness to this freedom. The short final four mile stretch (p. 117) whose blueprints endured a sixty-four year hiatus, took four years to build, largely by the post-Napoleonic unemployed. The Sheffield Canal Company paid the River Don Navigation £11,000 for its Tinsley wharfs, and settled any differences with the Duke of Norfolk by cutting the canal south of the Don to serve his manor collieries. A century of negotiation and litigation to haul barges up from Doncaster was history.

Watermill users could be ignored. John Roebuck had been one of James Watt's early sponsors, and Huntsman was a friend of the Scot. In 1782 Walkers installed the first steam engine geared to iron and steel production. Their tall brick chimneys soon became a familiar mark on the skyline, replacing the leets, dams and overshots which had plaited each of Sheffield's rivers for the last 200 years.

Leader House, Surrey Street. Part of an eighteenth-century new town; now a museum exhibit glass-cased by concrete and tarmac

Pond Mill, River Sheaf, 1860. Water augmented by steam, the tall chimney of the engine's boiler ignores earlier forms of power. But it is still rural in setting

Steam engines cost more to build, run and maintain than watermills, but they offered virtually unlimited power in terms of force and speed. Not only did they free the work place from the riverside site, but capacity was not restricted by water-flow rates nor their variation due to seasons and upstream mills. From Huntsman and his two assistants' 8 tons in 1751, straight steel production could become the sole province of massive plant in massive works.

The canal basin ushered industry towards the Don. Perhaps the most significant aspect of the Globe Works (p. 117) is its name. It symbolizes Sheffield's international status, where production was geared to foreign markets, rather than products just happening to reach them. The United

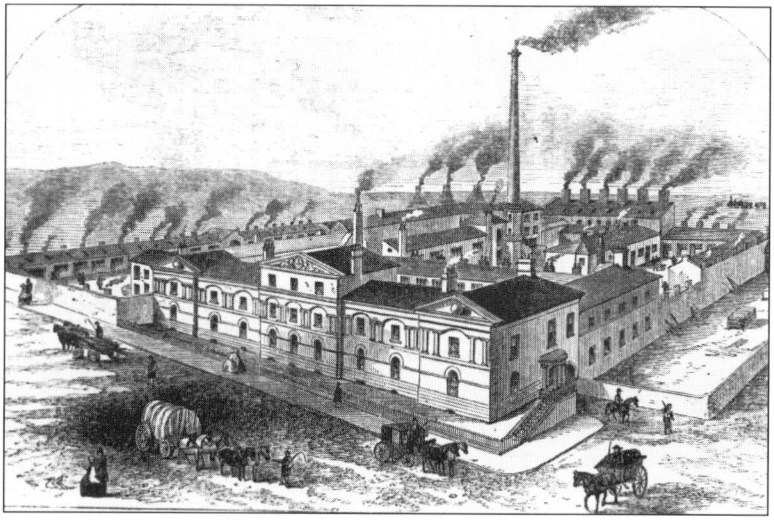

Globe Works 1863–5. J. Walters & Co. is still a single occupant

States was particularly important, and another green-field development, the cutler Wolstenholme's Washington Works of 1837, echoed this.

The Globe Works was also on a different scale to the preceding eighteenth-century workshops, if still small by the standards set by some cloth mills in the Pennines. Individual manufacturing processes remained much the same, but they sat on one site operated by a single company. These premises also included warehousing and offices. Clocking in and out for a weekly wage was fast becoming the norm. Yet the Globe Works continued the owner-occupier tradition, its pro-

Globe Works 1975 and 1990. By 1975 the subdivision into smaller and smaller firms is total. In 1990 the Works was refurbished. In contrast, the giant works of the Lower Don were never subdivided nor refurbished

1820s to 1990s. The Sheaf Works, perhaps the most elegant in Sheffield, awaits redevelopment – with its canal basin

prietor, William Ibbotson, choosing to reside there. At first a green-field site on the edge of town, the later smoke and noise of competitors were to change his mind. Its splendid architecture perhaps owes more to the deification of the work place, the Protestant work-ethic writ in stone, than to purely domestic style.

Similar in style and date, the Sheaf Works has no domesticity. Today it stands alone, awaiting redevelopment and divorced from its origins. It was built to fabricate tools from the steel furnaces immediately behind, obscured from town by its Georgian façade. Smack on to the canal basin, it was in the prime industrial location of its day. By 1838 the Sheffield and Rotherham railway changed all that.

Station Hotel, artefact of a lost line under Wicker Arches, which carried the line served by the Royal Victoria Hotel. Today it is the world's most elegant Holiday Inn

Only the Station Hotel and the humpback in Sutherland Street record Sheffield's first steam railway. It took passengers nine and a half hours and innumerable changes to reach London; the line was meant for freight, to service one of the most massive industrial developments the world will ever see. Works after works fed by its rails, the green-field ways of Attercliffe, then Brightside, were roofed, yarded and covered in soot.

Charles Cammell's Cyclops Works was the first in 1845, the other great names – Firth, Brown, Jessop, Vickers – were soon next door neighbours. 'I want to be a merchant,' declared the young John Brown, 'for a merchant deals with the world, while a steel-maker only with Sheffield.' True to both professions, his original Atlas Works of 1848 on Furnival Street was to the older courtyard pattern, more geared to carthorses and canal barges. In 1857 he changed with a vengeance, moving the name to a new works which by 1863 straddled both sides of the railway, and employed 3,000 men, ten times the number who could fit shoulder to shoulder in the 1848 courtyard.

'In 1843 every movement that really counted in the development of Sheffield . . . had already begun.' Mary Walton's words (p. 117) are absolutely right. Eighteenth-century delays in ventures such as the canal seemed to accelerate nineteenth-century expansion. It wasn't too difficult to survive the slumps which did for Parker, Shore & Co,

Atlas Works, 1865. Three thousand clocked in for John Brown each day

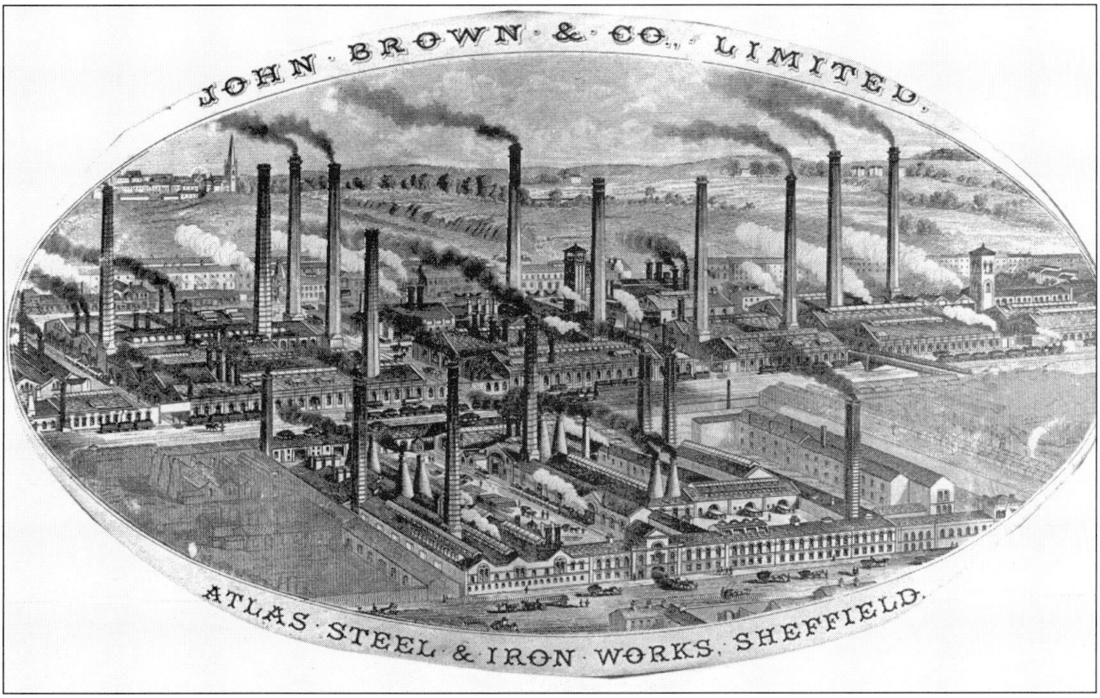

Atlas site, 1992. Nothing else survives; compare with the Globe Works (p. 61)

bankers, or electroplating, which knocked the bottom out of the Sheffield Plate trade. In fact those beginnings in industry were in train at least fifty years earlier, by 1792, before the Napoleonic Wars. Factories, high quality and quantity steel production, investment banking and market demand simply grew. They affirmed that the canal, railway and the Don would become steel valley.

Before they brought the railway to Sheffield, its Huntsman crucibles poured out 10,000 tons of steel in 1835, a colossal increase from Huntsman's original eight. Steel manufacture was no longer a service trade to cutlers, the two professions now possessed independent trajectories. In 1860 the Cutlers' Company admitted the steel-makers and engineers, and by 1873 their output was 100,000 tons. What were they making, as well as substantial profits?

The pre-railways trade focused upon tools but increasingly more basic forms, such as wire, and high quality metals for outside manufacturers. From a steel importer, Sheffield turned itself into a steel exporter, transferring its label of quality from its blades to their raw material. By 1843 it made 90 per cent of the UK's crucible output, and almost half Europe's.

The profits went into new works alongside the railway which would manufacture new products. The problem of shunting trains without harming the rolling stock was solved by John Brown's conical steel buffer of 1848, still used today. In 1860 Brown transferred his talents to observe the French ironclad *Le Gloire* in Toulon harbour. Back home he initiated research and development into how to roll steel armour rather than bolt on

River Don engine, Kelham Island Industrial Museum (p. 117). Three cylinders, each the size of a man, producing the power of two hundred family saloons is used to roll 100-ton slabs of armour, like pastry

hammered iron cladding. By 1867 his new Atlas works rolled out 75 per cent of the Royal Navy's protective needs.

Better armour leads to bigger guns with better shells, which leads to better armour. This war drawn up by ordnance specifications was fought between Sheffield steel-makers, to their profit. Machinery and products grew larger and larger, the massive River Don engine rolling foot-thick battleship armour. Around three dozen Dreadnoughts each displacing 20,000 tons were ruling the waves by 1914. That amount of metal would make an astronomical number of ploughshares or penknife blades.

Henry Bessemer's converter of 1856, once proven, was quickly adopted to provide the unrefined steel for the waiting crucibles. With the gift of hindsight some have said the steelmasters were slow to take up Huntsman's and Bessemer's inventions. Initially reluctant, yes, since they were unvalidated techniques to replace methods which already worked well enough. Once proven, though, they were soon picked up. Despite intrinsic transport difficulties and lack of good ore sources, Sheffield's adoption of the Bessemer converter led to diversification into basic products such as rail, with Sir John Brown lending his name to the Brown, Bayley & Dixon Works of 1870, now under the Don Valley Stadium.

In the other direction of diversification, completed products rather than components, munitions reigned supreme. Vickers, a name still active in the arms industry, could show visitors to the River Don Works ore coming in one end and guns out the other. Foreign potentates or War Office officials stepped from the Royal Victoria Station into a waiting carriage to order made-to-measure battleships or howitzers along Saville Street, as they might a suit from Savile Row. Sheffield was the imperial arsenal of the British Empire.

Bessemer Converter, outside Kelham Island Industrial Museum (p. 117). A question of scale. How many of Huntsman's crucibles (p.56) would fill it to the brim?

But not for long. As well as diversifying within the town, by the end of the century the steelmasters were investing their interests in other concerns far beyond the six-mile radius around Hallamshire which was the original ambit of the Cutlers' Company. Among these, John Brown's took over Thompson's shipyard on the Clyde; Cammell's amalgamated with Laird's to form the Cammell-Laird yard at Birkenhead. Firth's invested in Harland & Woolf, Belfast, as well as the USA and Russia, while Vickers went into naval yards at Barrow, gun factories in Birmingham and sired a lineage the god Mars would be proud of, still making everything from tanks to nuclear submarines. Following John Roebuck's interest in the Carron ironworks a century earlier, these companies are Victorian precursors of today's multinationals. The historical irony is that their origins are virtually forgotten or ignored outside Sheffield, and shunned within.

Fitzalan Square, 1900s. How many of these men patiently waiting for a tram to run on Hadfield's patent manganese steel rails would die in the trenches wearing helmets made from the same stuff?

From steelmasters to steel entrepreneurs. This expansion forms the first rationalization of Sheffield's steel industry. The boom into rail production rapidly went bust due to inherent transport difficulties exacerbated by more fuel-efficient furnace techniques. Just as Walker had moved Grenoside to Masborough after five years in 1846, by 1883 Cammell's dropped a ten-year-old rail plant at Dronfield for a coastal site at Workington. But the control of steel quality made possible within a crucible led to Sheffield's pole position in ferro-metallurgy. Robert Mushet developed a self-hardening steel in 1858 which was the basis for modern high-speed steels. This was taken further by Hadfield's manganese and silicon steels of 1883 and 1884.

Sheffield's bedrock became specialist steels. Siemen's open-hearth furnance of 1861 presented a more controlled initial product than Bessemer's converter, confining Huntsman's crucible steel to high-stress tool production. On the other hand, Gilchrist Thomas's 1879 process to render phosphoric iron ore suitable for steel production not only opened up the Cleveland, Lincolnshire and Northamptonshire geologies – Middlesborough, Consett, Scunthorpe and Corby – but also those in France, Germany and the USA.

This meant that Sheffield's bulk steel trade was dead in the water, while foreign nations could develop their own competitive specialist steel industries. When Queen Victoria pushed a button which ordered teams of men to open the gates of the new Town Hall of the new city in 1897, its steel industry had already passed its zenith.

CHAPTER SEVEN

The Turn of Two Cities

'The country between Sheffield and Barnsley is fine, it abounds with the beauties of landscape.'

Arthur Young, 1769

'All the way along from Leeds to Sheffield it is coal and iron, and iron and coal.'

William Cobbett, 1830

If you like history not to smell of roses, but sweet light machine oil, where growth equals progress and output prosperity, you may find yourself skipping this chapter, and the rest, not that they smell of roses. If you do, you'll miss what makes Sheffield Sheffield, and not just any other industrial city.

Young and Cobbett were the James Camerons of their day. In two generations they saw England change itself, and, unlike industrialization, these social conditions were irreversible. As Mary Walton (p. 117) says, these conditions were in place before 1843, but their origins are more diffused chronologically. From Daniel Defoe to Jane Austen is the critical period for Sheffield steel; for its workers and families it is Jonathan Swift to Mary Shelley.

During this period, workers and proprietors just free from direct feudal control became bonded to each other according to the dictates of capitalism. By 1843 this was already sharply pronounced, due to the relatively small number of employers with increasingly large labour forces, and without an intervening professional class. Although the steel and cutlery industries share similar technological and economic trajectories, their labour histories diverge because of the increasing size and power of steel companies and work forces. By 1843 there were no 'Little Meister' equivalents in steel manufacture.

The beginnings of this process reach back at least to 1700. The Cutlers' Company passed rules to permit unskilled labour in the manu-

Townhead, 1630

facture of scythes. If only in response to demand, and only for basic work, nonetheless this signifies a critical change from working for oneself to gain and use a skill (even though a William Blythe may order and distribute the goods) to working for someone else entirely. In economic terms a Little Meister who employed others was no longer so little. Today it dominates life in the industrialized world, but this was the start of the classic employer–employee relationship, the human element to match capital and technology in the construction of buildings like the Sheaf and Globe Works (pp. 61-3). Without workers there can be no factories.

As with all industries, from the production of books to breakfast cereals, there were good employers and bad employers, with most in between. However, unlike books and breakfast cereals, it was not a matter of taste, nor often of choice, although specific views and actions were usually defined by whether you sealed or opened a wage packet. Just as iron-foundry masters formed the Spencer Syndicate towards the end of the seventeenth century, workers formed benefit societies and sick clubs, which by 1720 already possessed the organization and power to call strikes against long hours. Their Little Meister fathers would have scratched their heads: they could as soon call a strike as sack themselves.

Although national governments were more or less against organized labour, it seems at first in Sheffield that their activities were tolerated if not encouraged by the non-waged of the day, from the landed gentry to the Church. If radicalism is questioning the *status quo*, the town's strong tradition from the mid-seventeenth century of religious dissent would have emphasized the rights of independent thought and beliefs, regardless of means. By 1786 Sheffield possessed fifty-two cutlery unions.

In fact the mixed factory/Little Meister system suited employers down to the ground. As cutlery was a labour-intensive small scale industry, the larger firms soon learnt to pick up and drop outworkers according to demand. When order books bulged everyone was happy; but when there were more workers than work, outworkers were competing against each other within Sheffield, rather than six miles beyond the bounds of Hallamshire as intended by the original precepts of the Cutlers' Company only a century earlier in 1624.

One way in which outworkers could gain an edge on rivals was by cutting prices. This in turn meant employers could cut wages to their own workers or offer them the sack. As their own numbers grew, the employers' hands were also forced by competition between themselves. The strikes for more pay in 1777, 1787, 1790 and 1796 by file, table-knife, scissor and spring-knife workers were decreasingly successful yet increasingly political. Both sides were influenced and polarized by the Age of Revolution, until what had begun as a quest for reasonable employment conditions ended as a perceived threat against the state.

During this process the Cutlers' Company found itself pulled every way but loose. Within its Hall were members from each side of the newly dug divide. If none quite knew which side of their bread was buttered, by 1790 they decided who buttered whose slices by supporting the employers in the scissor-workers' strike. With the outlawing of trades unions, individual workers were left legally powerless.

In the short term this led to extreme profits and poverty. Firms did go bust but there is an earth between being bankrupt and penniless – glance at today's Maxwell dynasty. The workhouse kept labour costs down, for it placed a premium on finding and keeping a job whatever the wage. As long as there have been factories in Sheffield, there have been unemployed.

In this longer term of two centuries, the suppression of labour-costs led to underinvestment in plant and training. The cutlery industry failed to keep up with changing practices. This led to the belief held by Little Meisters, workers and bosses alike that 'because the cutlery industry refused to lend itself to large-scale production, the trade remained very much a domestic one' (Edward Vickers, p. 117). This unduly conservative refusal has little to do with technology. It rested exclusively upon the uneconomic exploitation of workers: the clothes, shoe, print and brewing industries, for example, forsook their domestic origins at this time. Had Sheffield cutlery firms invested more heavily in their employees and work places then, they would have started to be more fit to match later German and other foreign competitors. By reducing labour costs to the bare bones they were slowly cutting their own throats too.

Meanwhile, their workers choked to death. Grinding was no longer a part-time seasonal occupation, just as we might occasionally sand wooden floors or insulate dusty lofts. Instead steam engines speeded up wheels, continuously driving their dust into the grinder's lungs. 'There is no more melancholy object than a fork-grinder looking prematurely old and dying from the dust inhaled in his trade,' stated Dr J.C. Hall, senior physician at Sheffield Public Hospital. Grinding commanded high wages, in return for lives cut in two by grinder's disease or *silicosis*.

Thus the worker/employer relationship became enshrined. The Methodist William Ibbotson, builder and proprietor of the Globe Works (pp. 60-1), declared in 1836: 'The God of nature has established a just and equitable law, which no man has the right to disturb . . . when servants unite to extort from employers, that share of the profit which of right belongs to the master, they equally violate the laws of equity.' God was on the side of the employers, even if the original Methodists would not have recognized the worker/employer relationship in the first place.

Needless to say, union activists were not over-impressed by Ibbotson's theology. They bombed his factories instead. This group was called Ratteners, from the original offence or threat of knobbling a (non-union) grinder's wheel. What they did was, of course, illegal; the frustration of their powerless position perhaps made it inevitable. Ibbotson did not need to have God on his side while he had the law, the press and the bourgeois at his shoulder. In contrast, the workers and their unions invoked a conspiracy of silence to protect those who did the dirty work.

People were killed. Just two and probably not deliberately, but from a barely tolerated nuisance outside the law, trades unions were now subject to a Royal Commission. William Broadhead, a saw grinder, publican and treasurer of the Associated Trades of Sheffield, was put in the frame but never found guilty. Instead, the Act of 1871 legalized trades unions, and disputes could be settled by talk and industrial action, rather than threats and bombs. Just as all union leaders weren't angels, nor were all employers fiends. William Ibbotson wouldn't share the milk of human kindness with his workers, but Mark Firth happily ate meat pies with his own. The local papers mourned his death in 1880 with black-edged editions.

Even though Firth's and the other large steel firms weren't to dominate the overall labour market until the First World War, the nineteenth-century division between employers and employees led to Sheffield being divided into two. First, the home from the work place. The poorhouse became the workhouse. Before factories Sheffield craftsmen worked near or at home, much in the same way that today a shopkeeper may live in a flat above the premises. Although areas like Heeley, Attercliffe and Darnall grew throughout the seventeenth and eighteenth centuries, they each retained an organic and independent village character. The intensity of labour became extreme; in 1769 Arthur Young noted women and children working alongside men, but in the same sorts of houses and streets as a century earlier.

Factories meant close-knit residential developments – back-to-backs. Intrinsically they were not unreasonable homes, as those who have bought the survivors in West Yorkshire will testify. Their notoriety arose from their density, combined with lack of amenities: windows obscured by neighbours' walls, a single tap and outhouse for

Townhead, condemned property, 1910

Central Sheffield on a Working Day—

and on a Bank Holiday.

SMOKE — THE UNNECESSARY EVIL.

dozens of households, yet foul waste seeping through the foundations, particularly down Sheffield slopes.

Despite the cholera outbreak of 1832, the indices of epidemics was lower in Sheffield than in some other industrial towns. The air was bad. It was bad by 1843 when J.C. Symons reported 'one of the dirtiest and most smoky towns I ever saw.'

It went from bad to worse once the huge factories in the Lower Don Valley belched into people's lungs. Up to half a ton of soot fell on to each house every year, some from its own chimneys. Düsseldorf and Pittsburgh, also steel towns, were judged worse in terms of sheer pollution output, yet the concentration of back-to-backs cheek by jowl with the factories at the floor of a valley maximized the damage to health. Babies could not be left out of doors.

> If at rare moments you stop smelling sulphur it is because you have begun smelling gas. Even the shallow river that runs through the town is usually bright yellow with some chemical or other. Once I halted in the street and counted the factory chimneys I could see; there were thirty-three of them but there would have been far more if the air had not been obscured by smoke.
>
> George Orwell,1937

So if you could afford a nanny you made sure you lived lee-side of the smog. Huntsman lived and worked in Attercliffe. The Firths,

The Turn of Two Cities, part II. Tapton and Fulwood from the air. Not a factory chimney nor back-to-back in sight. Instead tree-lined avenues link stately mansions

'Now you see it, now you don't.' This is what choked George Orwell's lungs in 1937

Browns, Vickers and other steel magnates upped sticks to build miniature palaces on the west side of town, upon the hills, where the old water wheels used to turn. They knew they were the inheritors of the old landed aristocracy, such as the Duke of Norfolk. Just as their waistcoat pockets contained thousands of workers, each of their workers' homes would fit easily into the portico of their own. A town of two halves.

Today the visitor can breathe little of this world; the Clean Air Act of 1956 blew away the smog, the back-to-backs were all gone by then, and the miniature palaces had become schools, offices and barracks.

Topography had determined the next social cleavage. A town where work was separated from home became a city split by the River Don. Nowhere in Britain were Victorian class distinctions so geographically stated. Mark Firth may have shared meat pies with his workers, but their children would never play together.

Orwell, an old Etonian, judged Sheffield 'the ugliest town in the Old World'. At the same time Betjeman judged Broomhill the best and leafiest suburb in England. They were describing two completely different cities.

United in the need to make smoke, employers and employees needed each other. There could be no fine mansions without back-to-backs, nor back-to-backs without factory chimneys. Only outsiders ever complained about the appalling pollution; without smoke the two cities would die.

CHAPTER EIGHT

From Rhetoric to Rust

Sheffield has never been short of something to say about itself – if usually to itself. The emergence of voices begins in the eighteenth century. After John Wesley stood in front of No. 5 Paradise Square in 1743, his largest midweek congregation found its own ways of delivery. The town's first newspaper, Lister's *Sheffield Weekly Journal*, ran off the press in 1754; theatre- and concert-going developed in the 1760s, and a subscription library opened in 1771.

Today these endeavours seem almost Ambridge in their scope and influence, but if limited in comparison to Regency London, they helped enable Sheffield to speak for itself. Perhaps the Ambridge connection is more apt when applied to their initial audiences – a small group of solicitors, doctors and other professionals, as unlikely to shape the business of Little Meisters, the Cutlers' Company or the Spencer Syndicate as today's *Westsider* magazine determines either Sheffield City Council or Development Corporation policy. Nonetheless it provided a forum for debate and change beyond the enclosed chamber of the old Town Hall and its unelected town trustees.

These seeds flowered during the Napoleonic era, and the town became united in a variety of radical causes. Olaudah Equiano, an Ibo ex-slave visited to campaign against slavery, although investment in Sheffield industry came in part from plantation profits. Lister's *Sheffield Weekly Journal* soon folded, but Joseph Gales' *The Sheffield Register* was both more successful and militant, so that by May 1792, 10,000 had signed a petition for all men to have the vote. The authorities quelled near-riots with shows of force – two people were killed in Norfolk Street on 7 August 1795 – but the overall feeling was radical enough that the *Courant*, a Tory paper, died after six years, in 1799.

As with most campaigns against tradition and orthodoxy, Sheffield's radical movement was an amalgam of different origins, agendas and aims. The skein common to all lay in the desire for openness and freedom to discuss and determine the government of the town. A rattener would hardly agree to wage-cutting, an employer with rattening, but each would find common ground in fighting to have a say in civic affairs.

Democracy. A large number of people wanted a say in running the town, but only a small number had it. The Town Trustees, Cutlers' Company, Poor Law Commissioners, Highways Board, the Norfolk Estate and the Judiciary (still a manorial court) were each independent non-representative organizations; small bureaucracies faced with the awesome task of providing for a population which almost doubled every other generation, in a town which swallowed up its hinterland and villages. The consequent absence of coherent policy and practice (not to mention the unbridled presence of self and class interests) led to the building of a magnificent new infirmary in 1792, while thirteen women shared eight beds in one room of the old workhouse.

These situations were common enough throughout Britain; the problems of government were exacerbated in Sheffield by both its rate of growth and diversity of institutions. Each obdurate in survival, it was a hard task that Sheffield members of the Chartist Movement gave themselves.

In the same way that its industrialists were developing links and offices beyond Hallamshire, Sheffield's radicals now partook in national movements of empowerment. Eighteenth-century debating clubs and Whiggishly radical newsprint drowned under the *vox populi*. Ebenezer Elliot's *Corn Law Rhymes* of 1831 stirred ordinary people in Yorkshire and elsewhere, in a way not emulated by the revolutionary Lord Byron or any other English poet. Elliot died a moderately wealthy metal merchant in 1849, yet Sheffield workers paid for his bronze to be erected in the 1854 market-place. Their radicalism was now a tradition and heritage.

Ebenezer Elliot, speechless in Weston Park: perhaps Britain's most politically influential poet

The workers were not merely organized, they wished to affect municipal decisions. In the Reform General Election of 1832, the initial poll was conducted by the master cutler. Shows of hands, sealed ballots and another 'near-riot', when five died from army musket balls, demonstrated the clamorous need for reform, if only electoral. That agreed, the debate, as in post-Glasnost Russia, focused upon the pace of reform. Moderates preferred to wait; more radical or impatient Chartists planned to act. In Sheffield a stillborn people's uprising against their town rule ended with its organizer Samuel Holberry in court. Conspiracy and caches of arms were presented as crown evidence, but given the militia's reactions to demonstrations in 1795 and

Samuel Holberry's gravestone

SACRED
to the Memory of
SAMUEL HOLBERRY,
WHO AT THE EARLY AGE OF 27 DIED
IN YORK CASTLE, AFTER SUFFERING
AN IMPRISONMENT OF 2 YEARS AND 3
MONTHS JUNE 21ST 1842.
FOR ADVOCATING WHAT TO HIM APPEARED,
TO BE THE TRUE INTEREST OF THE PEOPLE OF
ENGLAND.
VANISH'D IS THE FEVERISH DREAM OF LIFE:
THE RICH AND POOR FIND NO DISTINCTION HERE,
THE GREAT AND LOWLY END THEIR CARE AND STRIFE
THE WELL BELOVED MAY HAVE AFFECTIONS TEAR.
BUT AT THE LAST, THE OPPRESSOR AND THE SLAVE
SHALL EQUAL STAND BEFORE THE BAR OF GOD,
OF HIM, WHO LIFE, AND HOPE, AND FREEDOM GAVE,
TO ALL THAT THRO' THIS VALE OF TEARS HAVE TROD.
LET NONE THEN MURMUR AGAINST THE WISE DECREE
THAT OPEN'D THE DOOR, AND SET THE CAPTIVE FREE
ALSO OF SAMUEL JOHN, HIS SON, WHO
DIED IN HIS INFANCY.

1832, the outcome would have been bloody enough in any case. Holberry went down for three years and he died a martyr after two, aged twenty-seven, receiving a hero's grave.

1843: the end of Holberry's sentence, and Sheffield gained its borough charter. At first the town council was merely a change in name only: having fought hard for seats in the Town Hall, the councillors seemed at a loss as to what they should do, beyond sitting in them. For example, the Royal Agricultural Society asked the Council for an invitation to Sheffield for their 1847 show. Due to a lack of beds the offer was rejected and an opportunity to surmount geographical isolation was lost. 'Destination Sheffield', the welcoming city, had another 150 years to wait.

More urgently, a year earlier the health committee had rolled up its sleeves and commissioned a report, in which James Haywood concluded:

> Better constructed dwellings, both as regards light and ventilation, and a liberal supply of water; the substitution of water closets for the present open privies, and as many as possible of them in relation to the number of houses; also more spacious and commodious yards, well-paved and drained, with public washing-houses and baths in populous districts – and above all, places for proper and rational recreation.

The report was filed. In 1853, while conditions went from bad to worse, the health committee reduced its numbers, as its perceived duties were so light. In its infancy the Council soon learnt the habit of being able to say 'no', even, or especially, to each other. As Walton (p. 117) succinctly puts it: 'The vigour of the individual committees about their own subjects, and the apathy of the council as a whole about all the separate committees' schemes, is peculiar and rather amusing.'

Local cynics may well ask 'was it ever thus?' but once more the conditions for change were defined, indeed, this definition was fought for, yet a hiatus preceded the enactment of the change. During this twenty-year gap the radical spirit of Chartism ebbed into municipal pride. The thoroughgoing industrialist Sir John Brown became mayor in 1861 and 1862, and when the Queen came to open the new Town Hall in 1897, the *city's* chains of office rested upon the shoulders of the Duke of Norfolk. Samuel Holberry must have stopped revolving in his grave.

On the council's Monopoly board the worker's boot lost out to the west side professional's top hat. The Church, still divided between Anglican and Nonconformist faiths, in a mixture of drift and shove steadily dropped out of civic concerns, to the detriment of all. If the 1980s and '90s are all about privatization, then the 1880s and '90s equivalent was municipalization.

The tragedy of the Sheffield Flood encapsulated this process. As the town grew larger its water supply network fingered further west: Barker's Pool gave the fifteenth-century denizens their monthly scrub, by the nineteenth century a rural ring of reservoirs served increased needs, the picturesque boating lake north of the university the sole wet survivor of four knuckle-shaped lakes splitting Crookes from Broomhill (see Leather's map, p. 57) – all privately owned and run. By 1853 they were surrounded by gardens rather than fields, and the Sheffield Waterworks Company planned a trio of reservoirs to tap the Loxley watershed. Hardly complete, on 11 March 1864 a spring gale and full waters burst the Dales Dyke dam.

It was the worst disaster in Victorian England: 240 people died in minutes, 4,000 households flooded out as roads became rivers without warning. No monument acknowledges the loss.

Compensation claims spelt the end of the Sheffield Waterworks Company. In 1887 the council took over. It also competed with the bus and tram companies, first as a provider of tram-lines, then directly. In contrast to the bus de-regulation of the 1980s, the Council controlled public transport by 1896, running the first electric trams in 1899, their cream and blue livery still well remembered and loved.

Power to their motors fell under council control in 1898, when it bought out the six-year-old Electric Light and Power Company – one of the first in the UK. The Duke of Norfolk sold his market rights to the council in 1899, ending almost a thousand years of manorial control of daily shopping. Parks, cemeteries and, in 1902, elementary education became a municipal concern. Outside the work place the council dominated service provision from cradle to grave.

They reshaped the town. The widening of streets and the construction of the Town Hall literally moved the town centre a quarter of a mile west, away from the High Street to the far end of Fargate, *outside* the original medieval town. In the grand civic pride stakes, Sheffield competed with other Yorkshire municipalities, primarily Leeds. City status conferred in 1893 seemed as important as providing decent housing for the new city's citizens. Although back-to-backs were banned in 1864, no schedule was drawn up until 1892 to replace any of the 28,052 already standing. Sheffield surpassed its Yorkshire rivals in the 1911 census count, and George Senior, Master Cutler, declared 'Of course I'm glad we've beaten Leeds.' Mrs Senior's and all Sheffield's mothers' views were not recorded for posterity.

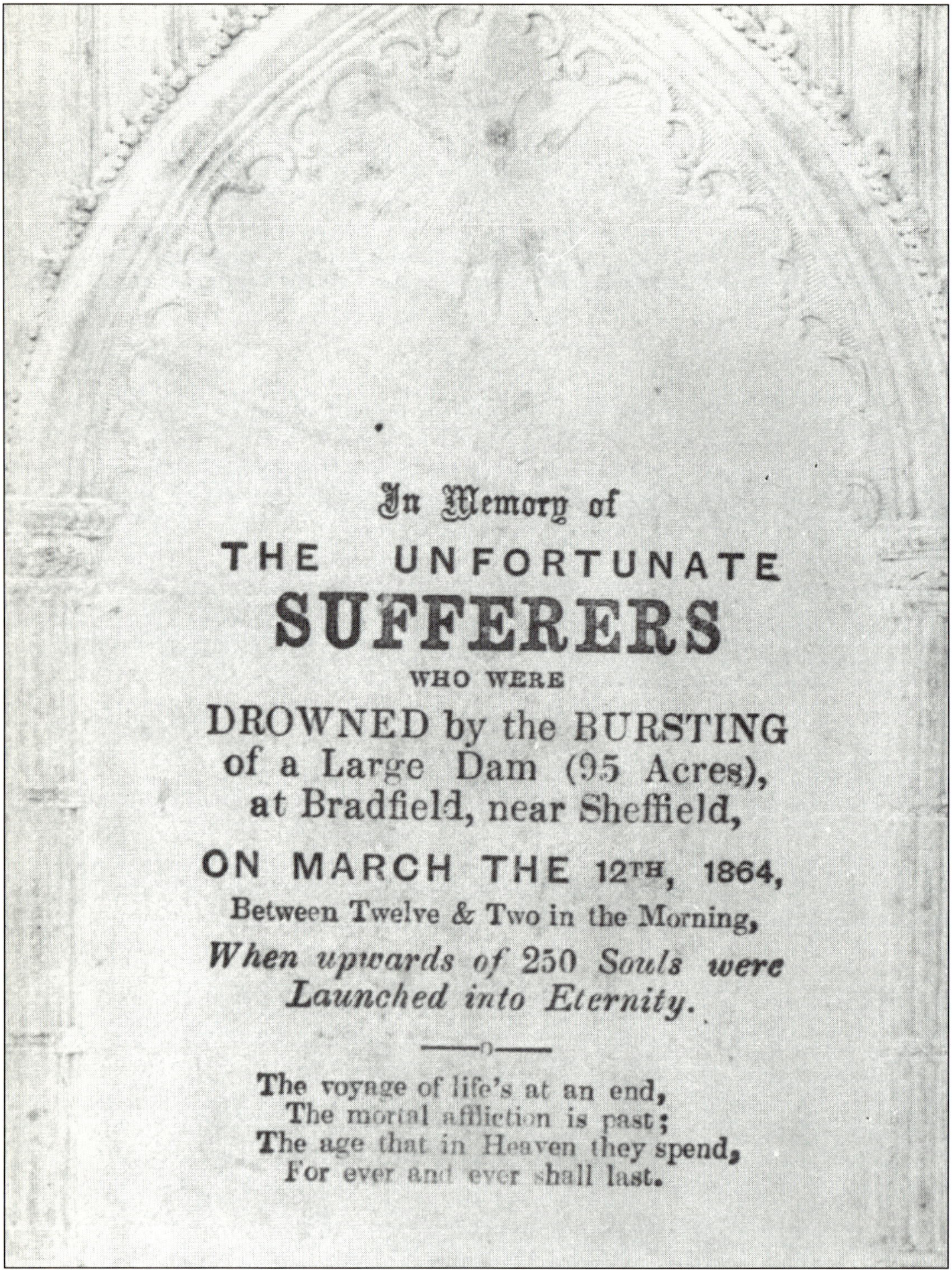
In Memory of
THE UNFORTUNATE
SUFFERERS
WHO WERE
DROWNED by the BURSTING
of a Large Dam (95 Acres),
at Bradfield, near Sheffield,
ON MARCH THE 12TH, 1864,
Between Twelve & Two in the Morning,
When upwards of 250 Souls were
Launched into Eternity.
The voyage of life's at an end,
The mortal affliction is past;
The age that in Heaven they spend,
For ever and ever shall last.

The city had grown to virtually its present configuration. Serviced by the Midland Railway, from 1870 the Sheaf valley through to Meersbrook became industrialized, and villages such as Heeley industrial suburbs, like Attercliffe twenty years earlier. Of the three lines into Sheffield only this still runs.

The old trams do not run now either, but they opened up the potential for commuting, answering exactly the same problem as tomorrow's Supertram. In the 1900s the council took over swathes of Derbyshire south of the Saxon boundary of Meersbrook. Norton parish was swallowed in red-brick rows of octagonal-bayed, shared-passageway terraces, as 'Sheffield' as the cream and blue trams which rattled people to work. Hillsborough, Owlerton, Wadsley and Tinsley were taken in, no longer separate townships.

How was this managed? The fiscal advantages of a single municipal authority were realized from the 1870s onwards. The authority set the rates. Primarily Tory administrations began the tradition of high rates, to pay for the quality and range of services, to a chorus of practised denials by politicians that they were high. Wages in Sheffield were relatively high, due to the high ratio of skilled workers. This led to an investment in people as great as the steel and cutlery companies' investment in their industry. Perhaps greater.

For all this immense growth from a small semi-industrial town in 1793 to a major European city a century later, Sheffield retained its discrete neighbourhoods, each with their individual character. In 1889 the first reference to its ubiquitous title of the largest village in England occurs: 'The population of Sheffield is, for so large a town, unique in its character, in fact it more closely resembles that of a village than of a town, for over wide areas each person appears to be acquainted with every other, and be interested with that other's concerns.'

Yet none of these villagers, from Ranmoor to Brightside, from Sir John Brown to the poorest buffer girl, would alter the village's reliance upon a single material – steel. Despite the rhetoric of overhauling Leeds at procreation, the city faced the rust of industrial decline.

This decline stood outside the classroom, like an invisible ghost wearing a dunce's cap. Sheffield's board schools from the 1880s were progressive and good, and the Council continued this tradition after 1902 until today, by a commitment to small class sizes. This was, and is, only elementary education. Initiated by Mark Firth's college of 1879, Sheffield developed a university by 1905. Primarily a research and graduate training wing for the steel industry, it enabled metallurgi-

Memorial card from the Sheffield Flood

THE KING

Carlton Villas, Firth Park and classic turn of century Sheffield. Brick and wood ground-floor bay, attic bedroom and side entrance, usually terraced with offshot kitchen, this example is larger than average

cal inventions such as Harry Brearley's stainless steel in 1919 to be exploited rapidly.

The classroom gap lay in between. The apprenticeship system provided a man with a trade rather than an education. In Sheffield, from shop floor to boardroom men were second to none at making anything from steel, from gun turrets to rat-tailed files. They lagged behind in putting those bits together – component assembly – and selling them. Alderman J.G. Graves is famous in Sheffield for bequeathing the Graves Art Gallery and Park. Few authorities acknowledge he made his name and money with a mail-order business. Commercially many Sheffield manufacturers acted as though goods sold themselves. By not assessing the market, the steel industry became vulnerable and over-reliant upon large traditional customers, such as the Forces with armaments and institutions with cutlery.

Unlike the Browns, Firths, Cammells and Vickers, who diversified across the country and abroad, the companies left in the Don Valley stuck to manufacturing bits of steel. Six firms started making cars before and after the First World War, but production failed with the depression. Some say this is because Sheffield labour was too skilled merely to assemble components; the Midlands firms, such as BSA who moved from rifles to motorbikes, lacked workmanship. No one in Birmingham agrees with this thesis. Indeed, the last Sheffield carmaker, Laycocks, successfully transferred to transmissions, and if you can bolt together a gearbox, you can bolt together the rest of the car. The Sheffield apprentice system, though, was ultra-conservative; for management and unions a skill was a job for life. It precluded any possibility of retraining or skill transfer.

Difficulties arose when attempting to market products through a retail chain to individual customers. It wasn't simply a matter of Sheffield not possessing a mercantile basis and the outlook of a Birmingham: Morris succeeded at Cowley, a green-field site outside the dreaming spires of Oxford. Sheffield's geographical isolation predisposed it to a commercial isolation; the village atmosphere cut both ways. In Sheffield this was perceived as a problem rather than a challenge, still less an opportunity. Technologically the steel industry remained pre-eminent, but as a business venture it had grown into a dinosaur.

During the Battle of Britain, Morris easily converted his assembly lines to war, whereas so specialized had Sheffield become that its English Steel Corporation was the one place to make Merlin engine crankshafts. No one ever considered making the engines there as well.

'Say it with lightbulbs.' Coronation of George V, 1911

War protected Sheffield industry. Armaments were large orders for large organizations, where productivity was less vital than production. Sheffield products also competed in battle rather than at trade fairs. Commercially this meant no competition; their military market captive, the profit margin was assured. This encouraged under-investment in plant and training, and fostered an attitude that the old ways were the best. For example, the enormous bull's-eye transferring those tried and tested techniques and reservoir of experience on to aluminium forging or large-size plastic moulding was missed. Sheffield sceptics say its steel industry lost order after order because it ended up making Second World War products on First World War machinery. That was because it employed Victorian management and marketing techniques.

Rationalization and nationalization enabled some modernization to take place, but the overwhelming problem of training at all levels was left till last. Unions and management publicly blamed each other for general ills, each turning a blind eye to how the world and customers beyond Sheffield would judge their flutter of dirty laundry. Hardly the best of advertisements.

Manufacturers make products from components. When demand drops they order fewer components and stockpile products. If demand flips back, their stockpile needs to be cleared first. Reliance on the manufacture of basic components, such as crankshafts, meant Sheffield's economy felt manufacturing down-turns first and pick-ups last.

Overall, even by the First World War, the Don Valley was an economic disaster waiting to happen. Viewed in this light, it is a wonder that Steel City survived as well as it did for so long.

The First World War changed the role of women in Sheffield, but worsened everyone's environment. Gas and electric light meant factories could work round the clock, belching effluent constantly into air and water, not allowing nature a moment's respite. The earth itself of Attercliffe's green fields of childhood memories became contaminated.

Shift work meant more workers, with fewer men in the city. Before 1914 most women worked in service. In other words they did housework, and weren't seen as workers in the same way as men. The broadening of work opportunities meant that Sheffield industry was still a man's world but no longer exclusively. Women also filled offices, and in some ways became less tied to the extremely limited range of jobs available to men. In terms of city partnerships, the first was between the sexes – and forged to end the war to end all wars.

The land fit for heroes lay littered with crippled ex-soldiers forced to beg. Industries geared for war were equally at a loss to deal with

'It takes two to tango.' Picket and policeman quickstepping outside BSC Templeborough Works for all to see, 27 February 1980

peace. Stocks piled up as prices plummeted; wage-cuts followed, then strikes and massive unemployment. The rich men's war had the poor up in arms. 1921 saw ugly mobs outside the Town Hall, presaging the calculated lawlessness of the Sheffield gang wars. National and local politics switched from a Conservative/Radical dichotomy to those of the right and left, generated more by differences in class and expectations than philosophical belief. Sheffield's strong radical tradition and predominantly working-class electorate led to a Labour council in 1926, which has run the city ever since, bar the briefest of reactions to Ramsay MacDonald and Harold Wilson in 1932–3 and 1967–8.

Grandiose socialist dreams were stymied by the Great Depression. This devastated a weakened cutlery industry, dramatically reducing the numbers of Little Meisters, until it became a specialist trade making quality material to order – as it had until Regency times. Coal-mining shrank away east. The heavy trades survived better, partly through amalgamation, and partly through focusing on specialized steels, so that by 1976 Sheffield made just 5 per cent of UK steel but nearly 50 per cent of sales. One of these products, stainless steel, enabled the mass-production of reasonable quality domestic ware, and Harry Brearley's invention unwittingly stabbed in the back the traditional cutler.

This decline of small concerns left a gap between employers and employees. Politically, debates became more polarized, and the two-city division between east and west was further entrenched. If Labour administrations levied high rates, they provided services second to none. The City Hall (1932), the Central Library (1934) and the City

Museum (1937) were showpieces for the provisions which extended from the oldest park bench or reading room to the bright new redbrick schools and council estates of the 1930s. Westminster placed city hospitals under council control in 1929, so all but employment was the responsibility of the Town Hall. The nineteenth-century industrial barons may have styled themselves on their feudal predecessors, but in terms of civic power, Sheffield City Council in 1939 at least equalled the strength of the de Lovelots, Furnivals, Earls of Shrewsbury and Dukes of Norfolk. Democratically elected, it also gained popular esteem: it was 'our parks, our schools and our council'.

The socialist dream seemed just a tram-ride round the corner.

CHAPTER NINE

The Politics of Culture

Darkness insists that Sheffield is a city, a metropolis; daylight reduces it to its component parts, to a series of bloated villages, unfolding across the undulations, linked only by sewers and roads.

Perhaps this is all Sheffield has become: an infrastructure in search of a city, a system of services and administrative units sprawling across an intractable landscape.

Richard Burns, The *Guardian*, 1991.

'Believe me when I say Sheffield is about to become the envy of every major city in the country.'

The *Guardian*, 1992

Culture is how people choose to live within the physical conditions they inherit. It can be defined as narrowly as Radio Three's waveband, or be as universal as an anthropologist studying an entire society. Different people possess different cultures and different views of culture. After VE Day Sheffield people had potentially more choice of how to live than ever before, and possibly ever since.

Clement Atlee's administration put into effect the wartime plans for a national welfare state. This took control of hospitals away from the city council. Nationalization of the water and electricity industries took these away too. In terms of their own plans councillors held significantly fewer cards.

Steel manufacturers hardly knew what cards they held, being nationalized in 1950 and denationalized in 1953. This, together with the partial nationalization of 1967–81, is often blamed for the decline of the steel industry. The switches to and from different regimes didn't help, but years of the British Steel Corporation's overall loss followed by the dramatic decline of the privatized industry during the 1980s also suggests steel making had been propped up as much as destroyed by nationalization.

VE Party, Colwall Street, Attercliffe

Austerity marked the post-war decade. It is hard to appreciate this today, when credit cards have long since replaced ration books. The Sheffield blitz remained in people's memories while they passed bomb-sites and gaps in the terraces. The first signs of change came literally in the air. Tear-provoking smogs ended with the Clean Air Act of 1956. Perhaps because of the number of parks, and reduction in output, or perhaps because of the apocryphal siting of smog detectors on the other side of the hills at Fox House in the Peak District National Park, by the 1970s Sheffield could claim to be the cleanest industrial city in Europe.

Any plans to build a 'Socialist Jerusalem' were shelved until 1957. Or rather dusted off, argued about, modified and rolled up again. No one thought to consult directly with the thousands of families about to be rehoused. How they felt about moving their homes, streets and communities failed to enter the equation. Somehow simple humanity

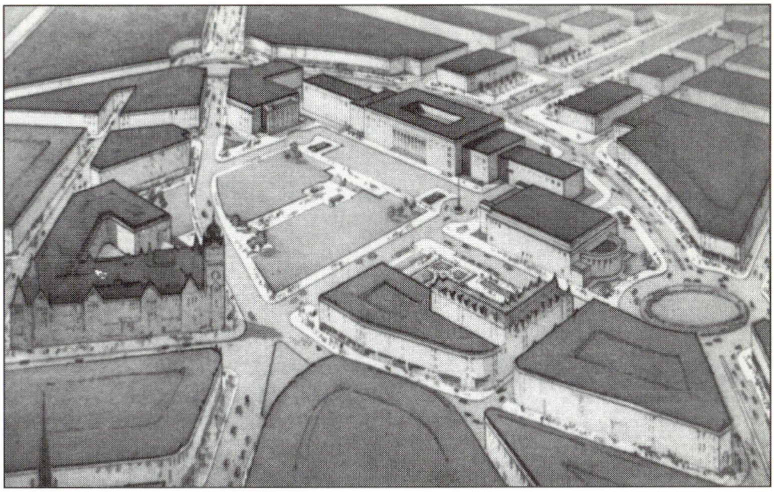

The Shape of Things to Come', *Sheffield Replanned*, 1945. Locate the Town Hall to appreciate its size

became divorced from inside Town Hall committee rooms. Planning proceeded with feudal hauteur.

The only people to profit were demolition contractors and concrete manufacturers. Development comprised two halves. First housing, where regardless of individual qualities, opinions and memories, entire streets and districts below the 400 ft contour line were compulsorily purchased and bulldozed away. From Darnall to Hillsborough complete communities vanished, including Colwall Street. Most houses were substandard and many beyond repair, while their residents were keen enough to move into modern homes without leaks, draughts and damp.

Traditional brick houses possessed a 300-year, albeit uneven, pedigree. In contrast to pre-war estates such as Manor, the housing department elected to build in pre-stressed medium and high-rise blocks. These promised to be both low-cost and enduring; inside twenty years they proved to be neither. The demolition of Hyde Park and Broomhall flats cannot be entirely put down to physical flaws. In layout they were terraces of back-to-backs tipped up on end. However good the aerial walkways appeared judged from above on scale models, in reality they became bleak isolated places, and when the lifts didn't work, the elderly and frail were left trapped. The habit of dropping by on someone while on the way to somewhere else, an essential part of the largest village in England, could never happen because the walkways were off everyone else's itinerary. Few complained of loneliness and isolation in the old terraces, but in the new flats it became a daunting problem.

Sheffield was the smallest of the major UK councils to invest and depend heavily upon these developments. It chose to rely upon the success of a single untried method to solve forseeable housing needs. The Gleadless Valley and Stannington Estates, which are on a lower-density semi-rural Scandinavian pattern, have more or less worked. Broomhall and Hyde Park must have cost over £1bn in construction, demolition, lost revenue and lost value of housing stock, while the cost of living on the Kelvin Estate should not be calculated in financial terms. It is no coincidence that a city relying upon a single industry should choose a single form of housing.

Steps, steps, steps. Old residents come to terms with new residences at Pyebank, Pitsmoor Road

The other half of the plan involved the city centre. Unlike the estates, which went up, failed and came down again, the central redevelopment of *Sheffield Replanned* never left the drawing board. Bits of dual-carriageway did not join up with other bits of dual-carriageway so that Sheffield has all the disadvantages of a ring-road and none of its advantages. Eyre Street/Arundel Gate is now called the Berlin Wall by today's planners because of the way it severs the centre in two (p. 91). Within this fractured structure different departments fought for different solutions. Planning wanted roads to go under pavements at the notorious Hole-in-the-Road or Castle Square which was opened in 1967, while Highways wanted a pedestrian underpass. Compromise was reached at Furnival Square, where traffic runs above and below the sandwiched pedestrian.

The tramlines disappeared under the concrete, and in their place buses provided an affordable and reliable service, while traffic flowed freely enough around a road system that Heath Robinson would have scratched his head at. Betjeman and Pevsner would have hung their heads at the modernist city centre. It never had a good reputation for architecture. *The Builder* of 1897 censored the late Victorian developments focused around the Town Hall for lacking coherence and detail. The individuality of communities, the village feel, hardly meshed with urban planning on the Bath or Edinburgh scale. But equally villages tend to grow piecemeal, reflecting the past, and the 1880-1901 developments more or less respected that. Not so 1957–92.

Ever since its castle became a quarry in 1648 after the English Civil War, Sheffield has delighted in flattening its past. Perhaps brick was associated, if subconsciously, with grim factories and back-to-backs, and the new Sheffield wanted nothing to do with the old. But council plans erased street patterns, notably around the Ponds, which had they been footpaths would have had droves of thick-socked walkers up in arms. As it was, post-war development seems a running battle between the Planning Department and the Hallamshire Historic Buildings Society, where isolated victories such as Leader House (p. 58) and The

Furnival Square looking east. *Sheffield Replanned* in reality: alienation and graffiti waiting to happen

Queen's Head (p. 37) stand as statues rather than buildings. The Lyceum Theatre, a great success since restoration in 1990, was saved by central government from council demolition. Not so the Ecclesall Co-op, finest art-deco, and arguably Sheffield's most important contribution to the nation's architectural heritage – a monument to the Co-operative Movement. It was replaced in 1992 by just another anonymous Sub-Romanesque Safeways. But for consecrated ground, the cathedral may not have been safe.

Often buildings went without replacement. Sheffield's scatter of 'bomb-site' car-parks arose a generation after Goering's worst.

The Royal Hospital on West Street was car-parked in 1978, just as the MSC brick ziggurat at Moorfoot went up. No one stopped to consider that the old Royal could become the new MSC. Listed bits such as the Mount Zion chapel façade on Westfield Terrace remain: in terms of architectural ecology, the effect is to keep an Adam fireplace but to destroy the Georgian Square.

Which building would you save? Until 1990 the Sheffield & Ecclesall Co-op faced the Telephone Exchange opposite, still firm favourite for the city's ugliest building competition

Or buildings were abandoned without re-use. The old Division Street fire station has been vacant for four years since the red engines and slippery poles moved to the new station on Wellington Street in 1988: ten years from initial planning to find a use for a valuable central city site. Orchard Square epitomizes the Prince Charles or Laura Ashley tradition of small-scale mock-bucolic nostalgia, but is a landmark for Sheffield town planning and architecture. The city's first coordinated retail development, rather than just individual shops, it also acknowledges the features and feelings of the past.

The pre-1957 centre was more interesting and convivial to visitor and local than today's. What went wrong? How did the great post-war plan finish up looking like a play-group squabble over a Lego set? Of course it's happened elsewhere, Derby on a smaller scale for example, but not everywhere: Chesterfield's centre retains its medieval layout, as do Bradford and Halifax, while Leeds has its Victorian grandeur. Sheffield has virtually lost the lot. It is easy, yet true, to say planning is too important to leave to planners.

Just as the city is a number of small communities, its council became another community, where individual departments competed as much as co-operated, a Town Hall culture virtually divorced from its townsfolk. A hamlet apart from the largest village in England, Sheffield politics were too often in the finest tradition of the parish pump. The best intentions became the worst of acts. Wholescale movement of communities into high-rise flats and the wholescale demolition of the city centre is one and the same: government of the people, arguably for those people, but not by those people. Inadvertently, in a city proud of its radical tradition, Sheffield's Labour council developed a form of elected dictatorship long before Mayoress Enid Hattersley's son Roy accused Margaret Thatcher of the same crime in the House of Commons. Worse, people started to speak of 'the council', not 'our council'.

If inter-departmental schisms ravaged the city's fabric, it provided the cause and means for excellent services. Parks, museums, art galleries, libraries and buses were the city's pride and citizen's right to use and expect. The less prominent resources, from community education to support for the elderly, were equally well developed, even if ratepayers on the west side of the city perceived the relatively high rates as a form of wealth-redistribution.

By the end of the 1970s there wasn't much wealth left. The 1974 establishment of metropolitan county councils was geared to reducing bureaucracy; it increased it. The South Yorkshire County Council wasn't socialist, a republic nor really South Yorkshire – as Sheffield, Rotherham, Barnsley and Doncaster pulled their own ways. A chance to co-ordinate services was missed; a true Socialist Republic of South Yorkshire may have achieved something, but the reality behind Fleet Street's paper tiger didn't.

The decline of the UK's manufacturing base (the three-day week punctuated with amalgamations, closures, multi-national take-overs and strikes) meant the slump in the UK-marketed steel industry during the 1970s and '80s was irreversible. Sheffield, being a specialist producer, didn't do too badly compared to bulk steel towns such as

The Republic of South Yorkshire – where women never supped pints?

Rotherham and worst of all, Consett. Even today around 20,000 people still work in the steel industry. The big firms have gone – none remaining match the 3,000 workers that Sir John Brown had in his waistcoat by 1863. Yet its products still command a good reputation for quality, even if they have difficulties finding the right customer.

Industrial decline hurt Sheffield's ethos as much as its economy. How could the industry which had created the city since Chaucer's day fail it now? Its identity was weakened. Everyone had lumped the cutlery and the steel trade, Chaucer's 'thwitel' and Brearley's stainless steel together, to conjure a picture of steel mills rolling since Domesday. This made it still harder for a conservatively trained and run industry and unions to accept that their difficulties were also an opportunity to move on; that the imposing works of Brown, Firth, Cammell and Vickers were but a hundred-year blip.

Management blamed unions, unions management; directors the council, the council directors. By 1984 factories were empty sites, yet still no one could agree what to save, as just one of the great gates of Firth's and Brown's original Norfolk and Atlas works was preserved to face the future in a sea of bitterness (p. 62).

The Clean Air Act of 1956 killed off George Orwell's smoke-belching monster of 1937. The chance for new businesses and visitors to come to Sheffield was scarcely considered before 1984. Again, the conditions for change were defined, only to be followed by a hiatus. By then the traditional rules of Sheffield's individual culture were virtually turned inside out.

From being a provider of services and the employees' friend, the city council found itself the city's largest employer. At the same time, their 1843 autonomy to levy what they considered appropriate charges for these services was axed by rate-capping. Their entire world was turned upside-down. In 1979 profit was a bad smell in Council Chambers; by 1984 it became the life-line to survival. At the same time the steel industry wasn't, while universal car ownership made the sanctuary of geographical isolation impossible. Only dreamers, fools or the brave clung to a radical past or future.

Behind the political rhetoric it took Town Hall one, possibly two, general elections to accept councils were to be facilitators and evaluators of services as much as providers. The learning curve isn't finished, given the budget set immediately before the 1992 General Election. This banked on a Labour victory, which meant that what was spent where in Sheffield was not decided by the people of Sheffield, nor their councillors, but the voters in the Midlands and South-East. A hard way to learn that politics is the art of the possible.

Reversing a dogma set by the Cutlers' Company in 1624, the city needed to attract outsiders to develop its infrastructure. The longest trend here is shown by the university and more recently the City polytechnic (aka Sheffield Hallam University). Not simply through research and industrial partnerships; student numbers have increased tenfold since Harold Wilson's 1966 promise of a white-hot technological revolution, and by AD 2001, together with the new single Sheffield College of Further Education, 100,000, or one in five, Sheffielders will be students of one sort or another. From an adjunct of the local economy and culture, tertiary education is increasingly a prime mover, capitalizing upon Sheffield's geographically central location in the mobile student population.

In the UK post-industrial map, Meadowhall is the prime retail example. Under the consumerist ethos of the 1980s – 'I buy, therefore I am' – old steel-mills were turned into one of the largest shopping malls in Europe. By the M1, it reversed Sheffield's geographical isolation by being a hour's shopping time from 10 million shoppers, and there have been 20 million visits since shutters went up in 1990. Inside a year it has exposed the vulnerable city centre to shrinkage and decline, where the former Cockaynes Department Store on Angel Street has waited redevelopment for a decade, since 1982 (p. 111).

It may have to wait as long again. The Sheffield Development

Meadowhall under construction: the Staybrite Steel Works deserted

Corporation, established in 1988, has a hard task: not simply to clear and develop sites in the Lower Don Valley, but also attract industry and business. Canary Wharf has failed spectacularly to move City of London companies half a mile downriver, so any success Sheffield has here should receive plaudits. In a trend started by Kelham Island Industrial Museum (p. 117) opening in the old Electricity Company buildings in 1981, Abbey National has taken over part of the old infirmary, Norwich Union at the Bow Works off Ecclesall Road, and Morrison's Supermarket in the Hillsborough Barracks complex. Empty old buildings are no longer a signal to rev up bulldozers.

A patchwork of demolition and construction sites, the Lower Don Valley is Janus facing the immediate past of steel and an undefined future. What isn't coming back is a local community. The children at the VE party in Colwall Street saw a wizard called The Future wave his magic wand and make their homes disappear. It seems perverse that their Development Corporation has no mandate to build houses in an area with immense community ties, especially when its equivalents at Docklands, Liverpool and Salford Quays did, utilizing the purely industrial waterfront warehouses. It might then have saved the elegant Jessop-Saville building, and it is certainly odd to find a place with pubs but no houses; while in the Mosborough townships there are acres of new houses but no pubs.

Speculative builders, identical to those in Norton a century earlier, have developed the Mosborough townships or Crystal Peaksville for

From square-bashing to Sunday shopping. Morrison's at Hillsborough Barracks

WINES
&
SPIRITS

Jaame Mosid Trust Mosque, Industry Road, Darnall. Home from home, no longer outsiders

the new home-owning classes. Young, they rely on cars to visit Crystal Peaks or Meadowhall rather than the town centre: a lifestyle inconceivable to their parents.

Perhaps the only area not to have changed significantly since the war is the west side. The scrunch of Shogun tyres has replaced the clatter of horse-drawn phaetons along Fulwood Road and through Whitely Woods, but the houses, road patterns and types of people remain very much the same. Personalized number-plates and natural wood conservatories denote as discrete a community as saris and the Jaame Mosid Mosque across in Darnall.

There is a difference: today's westsiders no longer depend upon eastsiders for their wealth. The east/west social divide is now a fossil rather than a function of history.

The city's cultural map also splits into two. West of the Sheaf and Don are all the museums, art galleries, theatres, bookshops; to the east the soccer grounds, sports arenas and leisure centres. Enshrined in council policy and procedure has been a schizophrenic philosophy that leisure and recreation (one department) and the arts (another) are two very separate things, as though people cannot possibly enjoy both jogging and theatre-going. The 'high-brow' has been divorced from the 'low-brow'.

The topsy-turvy career of the Crucible Theatre is due to this split. The arts are not commonly accessible. Sir Francis Chantrey, the nationally famous sculptor, only exists in books, and his work is not celebrated in his home town, where he chose to be buried. John

Ruskin is portrayed as an artist in the Ruskin Gallery, whereas his radical educational philosophy, which fired his art and set up two failed museums in Sheffield and the renowned Ruskin College in Oxford, has been shunned – at the terrible economic cost of losing an ideal model for training into the twentieth century and perhaps the twenty-first as well.

The Sheffield Festival attempts to bridge the divide for a month each summer, but cuts in revenue during the 1980s has led to an increasingly fractured arts provision. Local film-makers are encouraged to develop and sell their talents within the growing cultural industries quarter near the railway station, while at the same time the arts cinema closes down so that local people cannot see the films that local people have made.

For a century they've watched local heroes kick the ball or the opposition at Hillsborough and Bramall Lane. Perhaps this, and the Olympic successes of Sheffielder Sebastian Coe, initiated the 1991

Cultural industries quarter, aka the Kennings Building. As Elstree and Pinewood wither, will this help Sheffield become UK's Hollywood?

World Student Games venture. Hardly able to build anything else because of central government constraints, the Games gave the council a final opportunity, or excuse, to order concrete in the grand manner of their predecessors. The Games were a success, not least in enabling Sheffield to believe in itself again, and as a place the world comes to.

The facilities used in the Games are excellent, and should survive well after the debts incurred in building them are paid off. The Arena, Don Valley Stadium and Ponds Forge Baths each provide first class venues for major events and concerts. This is what the *Guardian* has other cities coveting.

More seriously, it provided only passive participation. The thousands who throng through the ticket barriers are a generation after the thousands who clocked on and off on the same spot. Regardless of cost, it is provision for the masses in the same way the high-rise flats were. You can pay to see world-class athletes perform in Sheffield, but if you yourself run in the parks, you'll find the toilets shut because of cutbacks. The individual is ignored, once again.

In the longer term, of lifetimes rather than decades, the most impact on Sheffield may come from its environment. It is one area where all agencies are agreed in principle, if not practice, and the Clean Air Act started a process to clean up the rivers, so that people now fish in the Don, and walk for pleasure along its banks. The South Yorkshire Community Forest will in a century return much of the original medieval demesne to varied woodlands. Provided cars can be kept in check, its greenness may eventually turn other cities green with envy.

Destination Sheffield is charged with attracting other cities to Sheffield, to cross out the 'Believe me' that the *Guardian* feels it needs to qualify its positive image of the city. As a partnership between the council and business, its motif is a 'welcoming city', which buys into the friendliness of Sheffielders, an undoubted attraction to individual visitors or businesses, without yet emphasizing the individual communities which make Sheffield Sheffield and add colour and depth to the initial attraction.

From these communities' point of view the single city standpoint belittles the opportunities Sheffield offers. The single city has been built by men for men. 'Whoever designed the Hole-in-the-Road,' a mother told me, 'never pushed a pram.' Women entered the Cutlers' Company in 1976. In 1992 the Sheffield Racial Equality Council, after twenty-five years' existence, reports that discrimination is just the same.

Is Sheffield 'an infra-structure in search of a city', or the envy of its peers? It can be both. Different people possess different cultures and different views of culture. As the Bengali Manju Chatterjee writes:

> Yet truly speaking I do now have a different identity. My soul roams about in the different roads and streets of Sheffield, it talks to my friends and remembers all the little things over there. In a single word Sheffield welcomes me. When I sit on my own in a quiet place I ask myself, 'What is the matter with me?' There is only one answer to this: 'You have a foot in two camps.'
>
> from *Barbed Lines*

Her words are true for all Sheffielders.

CHAPTER TEN

The Future

They don't make any noise. They don't make any dirt. They don't make anything.

Ernest Mills, from *On The Knife Edge*
Claire Jenkin & Stephen McClarence

In time all those who can understand will realize that nowadays things are being ordered differently.

William Trevor, *Reading Turgenev*

For children at school in Sheffield today, the steel industry and cutlery trade are history. How will they shape the future?

Theirs is a challenging task. They inherit a city where traditional conditions have totally switched back on themselves. No longer a secluded borderland or frontier zone, 2,000 years of topographical isolation have become a geo-economic opportunity. Already grasped by Meadowhall, the World Student Games, its universities and the Channel Five TV bid, how will ordinary Sheffielders react to metropolitan rather than provincial influences? Is the largest village in England about to become a myth? How will they react to work which makes no noise or dirt – when, ever since Mary, Queen of Scots heard the strange distant rhythm of tilt-hammers, they have dedicated themselves to doing just the opposite?

The population's means to define itself have shifted, altered shape and colour. From Board Schools to the 11-plus, Sheffield children have learnt to define themselves in terms of tight-knit communities and trades, to do with steel and coal. A straight-forward image and a strong identity. Today they can only rely upon a sense of community without quite knowing its purpose.

Outsiders are also learning to assimilate a different sort of city. Yesterday's smogs, the sulphur of steel, seem to choke their minds long after the reality has wafted away: 'Initial images are based on out-of-date perceptions of old style gritty northern cities, and most are pleasantly surprised when they come and look for themselves,' the

Sheffield Telegraph editorial writes, of the Norwich Union employees arriving in May 1992. In terms of image, if not identity, Sheffield has reacted quicker to its loss of chimneys and foundry sheds than the rest of the world. In its centenary year too many people will still picture the city as it was in 1893.

What will people see in 2093? Supertram will almost certainly celebrate its own hundred years, although by then it will appear as quaint as trams do today. It will have loosened the centre from the grip of cars, and attracted businesses to Sheffield. From Owlerton to Manor, the communities on the three routes – two shadowing the Don – will gain desirability for city workers, and the east/west housing divide, long since an artefact of smogs, will disappear. Fulwood to Beauchief will no longer be *the* place to live but just another pleasant suburb. In 2003 *Westsider* magazine may relaunch itself as *Sheffielder*, featuring the city centre which attracts visitors from Meadowhall. Graceful yet modern, the concrete dual-carriageways and Hole-in-the-Road will be in the past with everything from the specialist shops in Orchard Square to the Museum of Popular Music on Paternoster Row, an easy tree-lined walk away. Each year every community will renew its ties in the internationally renowned Sheffield Festival, when jesters, not misfits, occupy the Peace Gardens.

This picture, taken on a sunny day, is part of a film in which Sheffield succeeds economically. This will largely depend upon its ability to perform in the European arena, particularly with eastern Europe, which will either be a market or competitor. The same negative, developed under harsher conditions, doesn't look so good. If money is tight Supertram will be too expensive for most people. It will run minimal services to the point that its economic impact is negligible. It may even close. The east/west housing divide would continue into the twenty-first century.

Reality will be somewhere between these two images. Quite where depends upon how successfully the city competes with other cities for new business. There are two ways of doing this: either attract outsiders or support local initiatives. Outsiders such as Norwich Union or Abbey National have an impact almost immediately – the Development Corporation needs a major player. Local initiatives like the cultural industries quarter takes years. However, it is geared to provide opportunities to locals, whereas at Meadowhall locals fill the shelves while outsiders, at least initially, fill the higher positions.

A mix of each strategy ensures prosperity comes and spreads throughout an area. Here Sheffield should glance across to Pittsburgh. Both cities are built on hills, rivers and steel with tight-knit communi-

A return ticket from 1945 to 1992 (overleaf)

COMPANIES
DAVY'S

National Westminster Bank
EXCEPT BUSES
Lick yourself into shape.
South Yorkshire's Transport
SYT
South Yorkshire's Transport
SYT
South Yorkshire's Transport
70 DARNALL

Take the Supertram

ties, and their economies collapsed in the post-industrial era. Pittsburgh recovered to become the most popular US town by encouraging outsiders. Overall it does well, but the poorer communities have become economic cast-offs, connected to other places only by Pittsburgh iron kerbs, unable even to struggle as they once did against Carnegie's Pinkerton Men.

Sheffield would do well to ensure local developments are for locals. Otherwise the bleak view of 'an infrastructure in search of a city' will ossify into reality. The strength of community has probably enabled Sheffield to avoid any civil disturbances, which have made petrol

A string quartet for all to hear

A Sheffield Sunday at Mosborough

bombs a local industry on urban estates from Oxford to Newcastle in the early 1990s. It would be a tragedy for all were some parts of Sheffield to become no-go areas to others.

It isn't only a stark matter of haves and have-nots. The 1890s housing estates that are now Norton have successfully fought off a Tesco megastore; a prosperous community campaigning to determine its future. If on appeal the Tesco is built, Norton will find itself more like Crystal Peaksville, as the fabric of Sheffield communities becomes increasingly uniform. The South Yorkshire Community Forest will then girdle a Milton Keynes of the north.

If Sheffield is to retain its identity, it will be through the strength and diversity of its communities. Ignored in the concrete era from 1957, they have survived and often flourished virtually unrecognized. The home-grown ecology movement isn't woolly-minded in woolly hats, as Michael Heseltine pronounced in the early 1980s, but has worked hard to make Sheffield a better as well as a greener place to live. The Five Weirs Walk Trust has made the Lower Don accessible and attractive on foot; SCRAP has taken recycling into offices, and Healthy City 2000 helps return health from hospitals to communities.

These initiatives are vital to the quality of life, which in turn long term economic prosperity rests upon. Similarly the cultural industries quarter began as a way to help local bands record. If the red tape studios caused Norman Tebbit to guffaw, they signalled a change in Town Hall policy, to listening and helping rather than throwing concrete at people. This grass-roots or bottom-up approach is now permeating through the council, as is shown by the areas of special character in the Unitary Plan – the first time planners have acknowledged Sheffield as the largest village in England. An admittance by councillors that Town Hall bureaucracy has in the past resembled Prague's before its Spring may only be a device to soften job-cuts, and it is still too early to judge whether Sheffield Labour Group's 'Glasnost' will lead to 'Perestroika'.

A way of acknowledging and unifying communities, of helping them to discover, define and display their own identity is through the arts. The rift valley between the Hillsborough Kop and the Lyceum Crush Bar isn't bridged when there is in-fighting between Arts and Leisure in Council Chambers. Too often the arts are perceived as a way of bringing in visitors who will then unbelt. Big venues such as the Arena with big audiences are great for outsiders like newspaper columnists, but what do they do for locals who just want to read, write and perform?

The Sheffield Festival brings arts into the open, and if cynics say it is a cheap way of making a cultural splash, it is also a springboard for community involvement where every branch library or local pub is as vital as the café under parasols in Tudor Square. A festival which evokes both environmental and artistic concerns is an opportunity unique to Sheffield, a showcase for visitors and a delight waiting to happen.

'Cities such as Birmingham and Manchester are able to promote themselves convincingly as international cities.' *Towards a National Arts & Media Strategy* may not have heard of Sheffield. As a city in a country of cities it falls between the provincial and metropolitan. No motorbike dispatch riders thread through its clogged streets, joggers rather than muggers run in its parks. Despite its size, fifth behind London, Birmingham, Manchester and Glasgow, it remains a compact friendly place. A broader, more international economic base will help rid the devils that visit when order-books close, but the fundamental success of Sheffield is its people.

Communities from Brightside to Attercliffe, Ecclesfield to Ecclesall have retained their shape and compass since at least Saxon times, and have survived massive industrialization and municipalization. Each stands upon a threshold of change; its conditions defined by Sheffield's recent past, a century of monolithic steel and municipal works, now history. Today is a hiatus, not altogether recession-driven, but an opportunity for Sheffield communities to build the city they want for the twenty-first century. If their children flourish, living in their city of villages, then Sheffield will flourish too.

Introduction

A city of villages, there can be no canonical Sheffield walk. Before the 1980s virtually none were written down, but now there must be around a hundred, each for a specific purpose or locality. Most come from the heart. They reflect the pride Sheffield people have for their particular part of their city, and a wish to share with others. Tourist Information, local bookshops, libraries and museums stock the most popular and current, but the complete collection is at Local Studies, Central Library.

These three walks are geared to cover on foot the history covered in these pages. Each stands alone, but together they provide a chronological tranche west to east, from the Peak foothills to the Don passing beneath the M1.

Visitors will find their best way in is to follow the order below, but neither will you lose out by switching. They need no special equipment, but for the Porter and Don Valley do wear outdoor garb and sensible shoes, especially in winter. These also require bus rides, therefore pick up a route guide from any Tourist Information Office (p. 117), Transport Interchanges or SYT Travel Shop in the Hole-in-the-Road. Buzz their Bus-Line on 0742 755655.

Numbers in the margin refer to numbers on the maps. Distances and times are total but approximate. In case you run out of time, puff or the rain buckets down, included are options – marked by a * and *italics* – to zip you back to where you started. **D** indicates an extra: if you're like me, you'll find yourself wandering off the set route anyway. Enjoy yourself.

WALKING
TOUR

1: The Centre

(1 mile: 1–2 hours)

If you want to get into The Star, walk in front of a bus reading this book. Do take care, especially where pedestrian and bus routes cross.

Quietest on Sundays and early evenings, well-lit and safe, it evokes its past best at dusk, half-light raising unsuspected angles.

1 Open fields in 1434, and Mr Barker was finishing his pool to supply water down to a town where you and the Town Hall stand beyond its rooflines.

Cross to Fargate and notice at its far end how the Town Hall contrasts with the Telegraph Building's cream elegance. Just to its left, in the corner of the cathedral yard, stood Sheffield's first town hall, built 1700. **Stroll down Fargate**. This is a wide street which held livestock, rather than shoppers, for market.

2 Notice the narrow frontage between Black Swan and Chapel Walk, which follow the lines of medieval land divisions. The curve of Chapel Walk is a remnant of the old town, originally incised by plough-teams' repeated ambits, which survived the straightening and widening after 1880.

3 **Emerge at The Crucible's stage door and turn left down Norfolk Street.**

D **Right and into Tudor Square** for Lyceum and Crucible theatres, Ruskin and Graves art gallerys and the Central Library on Surrey Street, with Leader House opposite (p. 58).

Follow Eyre and Fairbank's 1776 planned Norfolk Street (p. 56) by continuing through the subway and in the daylight see how The Roxy nightclub and Odeon 7 are severed from Tudor Square's cultural complex by the 1967 Arundel Gate dual-carriageway.

D **Left down Flat Street** for The Hawle in the Ponds (p. 39) and the Transport Interchange.

Ahead, the Victorian post office dominates Fitzalan Square, whose open purpose is lost to buses bursting from the Transport Interchange, or what my nephew calls the Bus Zoo.

Keep to the right, and flick to p. 66, to see how the Square has altered since the 1900s. Behind you, Ponds Forge's chrome ventilators emerge like tail pipes from a Ferrari.

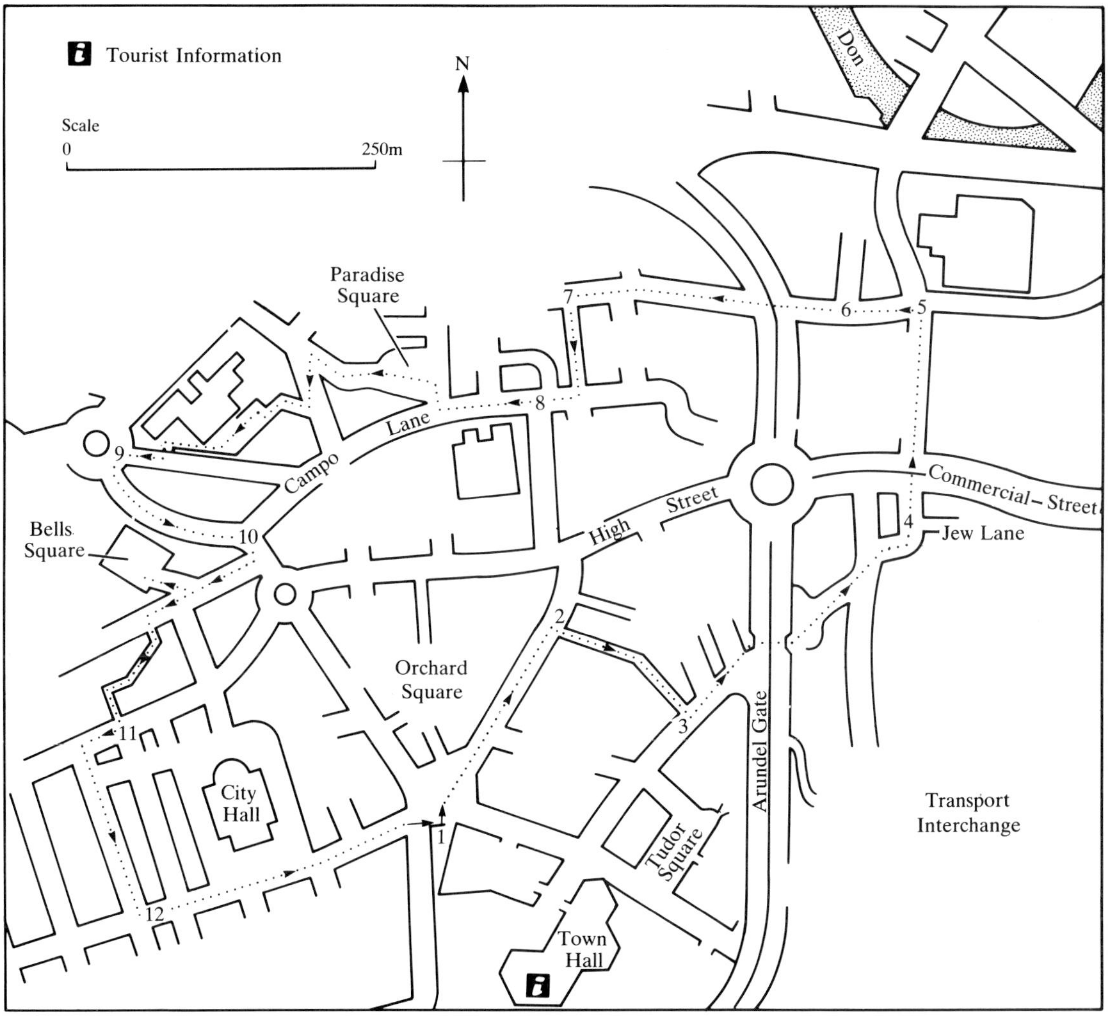
Tourist Information
Scale
0
250m
N
Don
Paradise Square
Campo Lane
High Street
Commercial Street
Jew Lane
Bells Square
Orchard Square
City Hall
Town Hall
Tudor Square
Arundel Gate
Transport Interchange
1
2
3
4
5
6
7
8
9
10
11
12

4 Between the gamblers' dens of Corals and Nobles Amusements is Jew Lane, dating from medieval times when important towns possessed Jewish quarters close to the mercantile centre.

Cross Commercial Street and dip down Haymarket.

5 **Turn right into pedestrianized Exchange Street.** Ahead of you is a castellated fast-food outlet. It signifies yet trivializes Sheffield Castle (pp. 34–5): Exchange Street roughly follows a 30-ft deep moat cutting the corner between the Sheaf and the Don.

D **When Castle Market is open, take the lift to the fifth floor and look north from a window.** It is 1300, you are Thomas de Furnival, surveying from the mighty tower of your castle and your domain is all you see: the little houses clustered about your walls, the fields beyond the Don, and today's concrete flats to the east your personal hunting park.

Carefully cross Haymarket between bus-herds into Castle Street. The Georgian building on the corner is now the Crown Court but was built as the new Town Hall in 1808.

6 Castle Street was known as True Love's Gutter, from a Mr Truelove, and signifying its pre-Georgian nature. Castle Green gives a glimpse of how Sheffield would have looked then, akin to the Shambles of York.

Past the Magistrates Court and cross Snig Hill, so-called from snigs used to arrest carts' and wagons' descent, their horses knowing they were in for a long clip-clop back up again.

The car park to the left and empty building behind were Cockaynes department store (p. 95), still waiting for redevelopment even before Meadowhall was a gleam in an entrepreneur's eye.

Bank Street, its name from Roebuck and Shore's first bank of 1770 (pp. 52–3), represents the change from a mercantile to capitalist economy, where high finance could be negotiated locally.

7 **Walk up Fig Tree Lane**, a typical pre-industrial narrow alley. Burgeoning Victorian population and social conscience are made evident by the plaque for the first Women's Hospital, 29 June 1864. Six beds were soon inadequate, and it was replaced by today's Jessop Hospital for Women (1875–8) – soon to be replaced in its turn.

At the top of the Lane turn right, and catch the Old Bank House where Thomas Broadbent opened his doomed bank in 1774.

D The clerics of St Peter's & St Paul's church may have taken a dim view of Broadbent's commercial acumen, usury being usury, particularly if they ranked amongst his unfortunate depositors. Their church became a cathedral on May Day 1914. Inside is a grace and serenity which belies its parochial origins.

* ***Slip up East Parade to take you back to Fargate.***

8 **Continue along Campo Lane**; turn right at Paradise Street into Paradise Square (p. 52). Apparently the most integrated part of central Sheffield, look closely at its shape and the mortar joins between houses to see that it is built in bits; from Nos 6 to 12 on its east side, Nos 11 and 13 on the south, and Nos 20/22 and 24/26 in the north-west corner. John Wesley preached across open fields from the doorstep of No. 5 in 1743 (p. 50), the Square a reality after 1777 as the date of the drainpipe-head to No. 19 testifies. This shows how different builds can produce a unitary effect.

Slip down Silver Street between Nos 19 and 20, turn immediately left up Lee Croft, then right down Sims Street and short-cut through the car park to Midlands Bank Pennine Centre, a far cry from Broadbent's 1774 financial house.

9 Down Hawley Street is three-storey Council housing dating from 1905, almost modelled on back-to-back tenements. Compare with what existed before at Townhead (pp. 68 and 71).

At the foot of Hawley Street, listen to Footprints's drop forge stamping out tool blanks. Imagine that noise amplified a hundredfold and you have the noise of Sheffield steel in its heyday.

Return towards the centre up Townshead Street.

* ***Continue straight on across roundabout into Leopold Street for the Town Hall.***

10 **Cross Townshead Street at the zebra crossing, along Pinfold Street into Bell's Square.** This typical cutlers' factory and yard were refurbished as offices in 1985: the 1987 craft-shops above Orchard Square include the same window design. Worn-out grindstones have been reused as cobbles.

Back on Pinfold Street, Walter Trickett & Co. Ltd Anglo Works awaits offers. **Cross over and find a tiny alley called West Bank Lane**.

11 This brings you out opposite Barkers. To your right is Mayfield House, a new office block for the Department of Employment; across the road is the Sheffield Co-ordinating Centre Against Unemployment. Each organization faces the same challenge.

Cross West Street at the Pelican, and stroll down Carver Street. The 1804 Methodist chapel will have soon changed purposes, as has the 1812 Subscription School. Whatever happened to *Sheffield Replanned 1945*? (p. 89).

12 **Left into Barker's Pool**. Admire the civic splendour of the City Hall. Think how much has changed since Sheffield was a village in Hallamshire recorded by the Normans in their Domesday Book.

2: The Porter

(3 miles: 2–3 hours)

The Porter is one of five Sheffield rivers, at present the most accessible with the Rivelin. In terms of water-power and industry, they, the Sheaf, Loxley and Don are fingers of one hand. The Porter flows through the history of Sheffield's west side.

Much wooded, this is a walk for ordinary misty days, especially in autumn or frosty spring. There are lots of ducks on the way, so take some dead bread. As well as ducks, there are swings, cafés and parks, so this is probably the best of the three walks for high-energy kids.

Take a 60 bus to Fulwood from the Interchange, Railway Station or High Street. Go downstairs as the bus dips down its first steep hill and get off near the junction of Brookhouse Hill and Crimicar Lane. Pause to reflect that you have passed virtually no derelict sites or old steel works.

Walk down Brookhouse Hill and right into Whiteley Lane, left into park and down to Forge Dam. In 1779 this was already the Old Forge, whose trip-hammers' beat may have triggered the name of Quiet Lane at the far end of Whiteley Lane.

D With a good map walk upstream to reach the Peak District entirely by footpath.

Follow the Porter downstream. Note the plaited interplay of mill leets and lakes, now bucolic serenity, two centuries ago an industrial estate.

Visit Shepherd Wheel (p. 42), originally Potar Wheel in 1584, with a Mr Shepherd employing ten men here in 1794. Look inside to see how knives were ground, edged and buffed; air thick with dust, dirt and sweat. If each mill employed ten men, over 1,300 owed their livelihoods to the turn of a wheel.

* *At Rustlings Road you can catch an 88 bus either to the centre – downhill, or Whiteley Lane – up.*

Continue along the Porter to Hunters Bar. The toll-bar in the roundabout was re-erected long after a ceremonial flinging from its hinges at midnight on 31 October 1884.

* *Almost any bus down the Ecclesall Road for the centre, an 88 to take you back up to Whiteley Lane.*

Go along Sharrow Vale Road, past Hadfields Garage and duck down Porter Brook View. Don't resist the temptation to look over the top of wooden gates, since behind is Wilson's Snuff Mill. As its picture postcard buildings proclaim, a wheel has turned there since 1604, but Joseph Wilson, a partner to Thomas Boulsover, switched to snuff by the 1760s. Still working as a commercial concern, it is closed to the public. The path brings you out at the General Cemetery gates.

D If you like how Victorian cemeteries celebrate death, give this at the very least the once over. Samuel Holberry (pp. 76–8) and Mark Firth (pp. 70–1) lie buried here.

Walk along Cemetery Road to Ecclesall Road. An 88 bus will take you back up to Whiteley Lane. Almost any bus down the Ecclesall Road for the centre.

3: The Lower Don

(2 miles: 1–2 hours)

Chalk and cheese from the Porter Walk, which largely ends by 1850, this highlights the subsequent years. Best on a clear day, take a pair of binoculars if at hand. The itinerary flexes between the city centre and Meadowhall, giving a free choice of start and finish points.

Take a 93 bus from Sheffield Interchange, Fitzalan Square, Haymarket, Wicker, or from Meadowhall Interchange. Get off when you reach the stop at Newman Road and Wincobank Avenue.

Walk uphill along Jenkin Road. At the brow of the hill, turn right and follow a cobbled carriageway past the 'Wincobank Hill. Sheffield Countryside Management' sign. Just beyond where the cobbles fork, you come to a low grassy bank cut by a more recent path. This is Wincobank Hillfort, at least 2,500 years old (p. 16). **Walk along the left-hand rampart of the ring** and spot the second outer rampart and ditch. In the Don Valley would have been fields, forests and similar settlements, looking more like the distant view behind you today. How many families would have lived here? No chickens (imported by the Romans) but goats and pigs would have scavenged in their yards. Despite bring the only hillfort inside the boundary of any city in the world, there is no sign to tell you what was once here.

In the midground the black shed steel works and the empty Atlas Site shroud an era. Behind are Meadowhall, the Arena and Don Valley Stadium, with the red-and-yellow reclad Hyde Park Flats a Brobdignagian SYT Mainline bus.

Walk around the rampart to a bench. Take the left-hand path, which is still edged with Penistone black kerbing. This rbings you on to a flat playing field reclaimed from the old tram repair depot. **Walk across on to a short ridge.** Compare the size of the factories with the houses: each black shed could contain entire terraces. Unlike the older westside, nothing here is built from stone.

Left along the ridge, down the hand-railed path into Beacon Road. Right and downhill. Left down Rothsay Road. Here are classic 1900s to 1920s private housing which replaced back-to-backs.

Right at the end of Rothsay Road into Holywell Road. A down-at-heel industrial patchwork ahead, but immediately on the right is The Grimesthorpe Family Centre, originally 'Brightside Parish Church Mission Hall & Sunday Schools'. Glance across the road to the overgrown graveyard of derelict St Stephens's parish church.

Catch a 93 for either the city centre – downhill – or Meadowhall – up.

The Next Steps

First ports of call for the visitor are the Tourist Information Centres. Sheffield has three:

Peace Gardens near the Town Hall, tel. 0742 734671; Railway Station, tel. 795901; Meadowhall Shopping Centre, tel. 569292.

To follow up the strands in this book, I'd head for:

Abbeydale Hamlet, Abbeydale Road South; **Bishops House**, Upper Albert Road; **Canal Cruises**, from Maltravers Street Wharf; **City Museum**, Western Bank; **Clifton Park Museum**, Clifton Park, Rotherham; **Creswell Crags Visitor Centre**, M1 Junction 30, A616 towards Newark; **Globe Works**, Penistone Road; **Heeley City Farm**, Richards Road; **Kelham Island**, Alma Street; **Shepherd Wheel**, nr Oakbrook Road; **Sheffield Manor**, Manor Lane; **Wortley Top Forge**, signposted after Chapeltown from A629 to Huddersfield.

Among the most useful books about the history of Sheffield are the following:

Barraclough, K.C. *Sheffield Steel* (Ashbourne, Moorland Publishing, 1979).

Hey, D., *The Making of South Yorkshire* (Ashbourne, Moorland Publishing, 1979)

Vickers, J. Edward, *A Popular History of Sheffield* (Sheffield, Applebaum, 1992)

Walton, M., *Sheffield, its story and its achievements* (Otley, The Amethyst Press, 1984)

Who'd have thought it? The Changing Face of Sheffield's East End (East End Publishing, 1990)

1993 is city centenary year, and a two-volume history will be published by Sheffield Academic Press. Around a quarter of a million words, it will not go back further than 1843. A third volume popular history with many more illustrations and far fewer words is also planned. Also forthcoming, a history of Sheffield's radical tradition by Simon Ogden.

Acknowledgements

In writing this book I have sought and gained the help of many people in Sheffield. Without them these pages would be duller as well as less wise. Perhaps more important is that they have given their help freely and openly, a simple instance of Sheffield being a welcoming city. However, any errors as well as opinions directly expressed are mine, and mine alone. For those errors I apologize. Sorry also to those I do not mention below: space is a writer's worst friend.

Thanks to: Gurjit Bachoo, Keith Crawshaw, Martin Olive and others at Sheffield City Libraries; Alan Bailey; John Barnatt, Peak National Park; Pauline Beswick, Robin Fielder and others, Sheffield City Museums; Nick Burton, South Yorkshire Community Forest; David Buxton, my editor and all the helpful staff at Alan Sutton Publishing; Steve Bond and others in Community Education, Sheffield College; Matthew Conduit and others supporting Sheffield Cultural Industries Quarter; Norman Fowler and Mike Morton-Thorpe, Education Department, Sheffield City Council; Melanie Francis and others at the South Yorkshire Archaeological Unit; Nick Gregory, Heeley City Farm; Jeremy Ham, Sheffield Unified Multicultural Educational Service (SUMES); John Heeley, Destination Sheffield; Low, Howard and Spink; Andy Myers; Simon Ogden, Land & Planning, Sheffield City Council; Alan Powell and Stephen McClarence, Sheffield Newspapers; Derek Riley; The Sheffield Photographic Centre; The Sheffield Development Corporation; Jude Warrender, SCRAP; and Cyril Wilson.

Photographs and illustrations on the following pages kindly reproduced courtesy of: 13, Dr P. Mellars; 18, D.N. Riley; 19 & 36, South Yorkshire Archaeological Unit; 21, Clifton Park Museum, Rotherham; 25 & 53, Sheffield City Museums; 27, 39, 42, 47, 49, 50, 62 (both), 65, 70, 73, 75, 82, 84, 85, 93, 108 (both), Sheffield City Libraries; 32, 74, 90, 106, Dept of Land & Planning, Sheffield City Council; 37, 40, 54, 63 (top), 68, 79, 87, 90, 92, 94 (top), 98, Sheffield Newspapers; 96, Whitbread PLC; 101, Dept of Employment & Economic Development, Sheffield City Council. All others by the author.

Finally to Kay.

Index

Except for specific places or people, this index is arranged by topic so, for example, railways come under transport. Italic numbers refer to illustrations.

Abbeydale Hamlet, *6*, 43, *43*, 130
Anglo-Saxons, 20–4; crosses 22, *23*; boundary at Dore, 24, *25;* place-names, 21–2
architecture, development, 90–1, 96
art and culture, 98–9, 107–8
Atlas Works, 63–4, *63, 64*

banking and investment, 53–4, 67, 112
Bishop's House, *48,* 130
Bronze Age, *13*, 14; dugout canoe, 14; Toad's Mouth clearance cairns, 14–15, *15*
Brown, Sir John, 63–5

castle, 29–35; Furnival's, 33–4, *34, 35;* 112; de Lovetot's, 29
coal mining, 43–4
Cutlers' Company, 44–5, *45,* 50, 67–9
cutlery trade, Chaucer and fourteenth century, 36–7; decline, 85; Little Meisters, 67–70; Sheffield Plate, 51, *51;* Tudor period, 43–4

Danes, 26–7, *26*
de Lovetot, William, 29
Development Corporation, 96

Elliot, Ebenezer, 76, *76*
education, 81–3; training, 83–4; tertiary, 95
environment, Clean Air Act, 88; environmental health, 78; Green City, 107; industrial pollution, 70, *72,* 73–4; prehistoric degradation, 15; South Yorkshire Community Forest, 100, 107
enclosure movement, 53–4
Eyre, Vincent, 56

Firth, Mark, 70–1

geology, 4, *5*
Globe Works, 60–1, *60, 61,* 117
grinding and grindstones, 4–6, *6, 38,* 115

Hallamshire, 22–4, *23,* 26
Hawle in the Ponds, 38, *39,* 41
health, 70, 76, 88
Hearth Tax, 50
Holberry, Samuel, 76–8, *77*
housing, back–to–backs, 71–3; high–rise flats, 1, 89–90; rehousing programmes, 88–90
Huntsman, Benjamin, 4, 54–6

Ibbotson, William, 70
industrial relations, 68–71; Ratteners, 70; steel strikes, 85
Iron Age, *13,* 16–18; Scholes Coppice hillfort, 16, *17;* Wincobank hillfort, 16, *16,* 116
ironworking, Blythes 46–8; in Hallamshire, 32–3; at Kimberworth (1161), 31–2, *32;* Spencer syndicate, 46; Tudor period, 44

Lady's Bridge, 29, *30,* 38
layout of city, 7
Leader House, 56, *58*
local community identity, 6–7, 81, 93, 100, 106–7; east–west divide, 73–4, 85, 98
local government, borough status (1843), 78; Capital Burgesses (1554), 46; city status (1893), 78–81; Charter (1297), 35, *37;* Labour control, 85, 95; municipalization of services, 79; *Sheffield Replanned* 89–90, 113; South Yorks County Council, 93; suburbanization, 81

Kelham Island Industrial Museum, 96, 117

maps and plans,1066, *28;*1116, *29;* 1497, *36;* 1736, *47;* 1823, *57*
Meadowhall, 95
Mesolithic, *13;* Deepcar, *11,* 11–12; Thorpe Common, 12; Unstone, 12
multi-cultural issues, 100–1

national location, 2–3, *3,* 8–9; highland and lowland Britain, 2–3
Neolithic, *13,* 14; Ash Cabin Flat stone circle, 14
newspapers, 75
Norfolk, Duke of, estate, 49–50, 56–7, 76, 78, 79
Normans, 28–9, 32

Palaeolithic; Creswell Crags, 10–11, 117
Paradise Square, 50, 52, *52,* 113
park (medieval), 30–1, *31*

radicalism, 49, 68–70, 75-6; Chartists, 75-8
refractory clays, 4
religion, early church crosses, 22, *23;* dissenters and Methodism, 49; mosques, 98, *98;* church and municipalization, 78–9; St Peter's and St Paul's church (later cathedral), 29, 112–13
reservoirs, *57,* 79; Barker's Pool, 110; Sheffield Flood, 79, *80*
rivers and hills, *3,* 4, 114
Romans, *13;* coinage, 20; farming methods, 18; roads, 18–19; Templeborough, 18–19, *19*

Sheaf Works, 62, *62*
Sheffield Manor, 40, *40*, 43, 117
steam power, 59, *60,* 65, *65*
steel manufacture, armaments, 65; decline, 83–4; diversification, 65; eighteenth-century, 54–5; factory production, 54–6; medieval precedents, 37–8; specialist steels, 66; Tudor period, 48–9

Shepherd Wheel, 41, *42,* 59, 115, 117
Townhead, *68, 71*
transport, canal, 54, *55,* 59, 130; difficulties, 4; railways, 62–3; Supertram, 103, *106*; toll-roads, 53, *53;* trams, 81, *82*
Waltheof, Lord, 28-9
water power, 4, 32–3
Wesley, John, 50
women's role, (or absence), 71, 79, 84, 94, 104
World Student Games, 99–100
Wortley Top Forge, 41, 117